True Principles o
Book T
By
Frank M. Caraveo

Copyright © 2024 Frank M. Caraveo

All rights reserved. No part of this publication may be reproduced, distributed, or transmitted in any form or by any means, including photocopying, recording, or other electronic or mechanical methods, without the prior written permission of the publisher, except in the case of brief quotations embodied in critical reviews and certain other noncommercial uses permitted by copyright law.

Table of Contents

Prologue 1
Introduction 3
1. What is Baptism? 5
2. Understanding The Lord's Supper 19
3. Empowered for Service 31
4. Insight, Revelation, and Discernment 49
5. Origin, Commandments, and Purpose of Divine Law 61
6. Embracing The Sabbath 77
7. Managing God's Gifts 91
8. Living a Christ-Centered Life 105
9. Marriage and Family 123
10. Christ's Ultimate Ministry 141
11. The Glorious Return of Christ 161
12. Life Beyond Death 179
13. Hope for a Renewed Creation 193
14. The Renewed Creation 201

Prologue

The journey of faith is one of continuous discovery, a path that grows deeper and richer as we encounter new truths and confront the ever-changing landscape of the world around us. Having laid the foundation in *Book One*, we now turn our focus to the principles of Christianity that speak directly to the challenges and complexities of our current age. As society navigates issues of identity, purpose, and connection, there has never been a greater need to understand how faith can shape our responses, guide our actions, and strengthen our resolve.

In *Book Two* of *True Principles of Christianity*, we dive into fourteen additional teachings that bring clarity and strength to the Christian Walk, particularly in times of uncertainty and doubt. These principles are not only vital teachings from Scripture but also offer a roadmap for how to live with integrity, resilience, and compassion in a world that often moves in opposing directions. Together, they form a blueprint for believers who desire not only to live by faith but to make an impact through their lives.

Here, we explore how Christianity's timeless truths intersect with modern issues, showing how God's Word is as relevant today as it was in centuries past. As you read, may you find wisdom, courage, and a renewed commitment to live out the Gospel, embodying the transformative power of God's truth in every aspect of life.

Introduction

If Book One focused on the foundational elements of Christian faith, Book Two invites us to look outward, considering how these principles apply to the world we live in today. Here, we examine teachings that call believers to engage with society with a compassionate, justice-driven, and resilient faith. These principles challenge us to think deeply about how our lives can reflect Christ's love to others and how we can respond to today's pressing issues in a way that honors God.

This book's chapters address questions that resonate deeply in our era: What does it mean to extend grace to others in a divided world? How can we build a faith that withstands trials and emerges stronger? How do we live as Christ's ambassadors, bringing hope to a world in need of light? These topics, among others, seek to equip believers not only with biblical understanding but also with a practical, actionable faith that makes a difference.

Throughout Book Two, we will explore what it means to live out the full expression of Christianity in our personal lives, families, communities, and society at large. As you journey through these pages, may you be inspired to not only hold fast to your faith but to share it courageously and live it vibrantly, bringing God's kingdom to life in a world that needs it now more than ever.

1. What is Baptism?

Baptism stands as one of the most profound and sacred rites within Christianity, symbolizing a believer's faith, purification, and initiation into the Christian community. This ancient practice, rich with theological and spiritual significance, marks a pivotal moment in the life of a Christian. It is a public declaration of one's commitment to follow Jesus Christ and an embodiment of the transformative power of the Holy Spirit.

In this chapter, we will explore the multifaceted nature of baptism, delving into its meaning and purpose. We will trace its origins from the Old Testament and Jewish traditions to its establishment in the early Christian church through the ministry of John the Baptist and the baptism of Jesus. Understanding the historical context will provide a deeper appreciation of its enduring relevance.

Furthermore, we will examine the role of baptism in the Christian life, considering its symbolism of death and resurrection with Christ and its impact on personal spiritual growth. This sacrament is not merely a ritual but a profound spiritual journey that signifies a lifelong commitment to discipleship and community.

Additionally, we will focus on how baptism is understood and practiced within the Seventh-day Adventist Church today. By exploring the theological foundations, prerequisites, and the unique elements of Adventist baptismal practices, we will gain insight into how this denomination honors and upholds this sacred ordinance.

As we journey through this chapter, we will reflect on the deep personal and communal implications of baptism, encouraging readers to contemplate their own spiritual paths and the transformative power of this sacred rite. Through this exploration, we hope to provide a comprehensive understanding of baptism's central place in the Christian faith and its enduring significance across centuries and denominations.

Baptism is defined as a Christian sacrament of initiation and purification, performed with water, symbolizing the washing away of sin and the start of a new life in Christ. This act, while outwardly simple, holds profound symbolic meaning that resonates deeply within the Christian tradition.

At its core, baptism represents cleansing. In the waters of baptism, believers symbolically wash away their sins, echoing the words of Acts 22:16, "And now why do you wait? Rise and be baptized and wash away your sins, calling on his name." This act of cleansing is not just physical but spiritual, signifying a purification of the soul and a fresh start in the eyes of God.

Baptism also embodies the concept of rebirth. This powerful symbolism is rooted in the words of Jesus in John 3:5, where He declares, "Truly, truly, I say to you, unless one is born of water and the Spirit, he cannot enter the kingdom of God." Here, baptism is seen as a rebirth, a spiritual regeneration where the old self is buried, and a new self emerges, much like Christ's death and resurrection. This idea is further emphasized in Romans 6:4, "We were therefore buried with him through baptism into death in order that, just as Christ was raised from the dead through the glory of the Father, we too may live a new life."

Furthermore, baptism serves as a rite of initiation into the Christian community. It marks the beginning of a believer's journey in the faith, welcoming them into the body of Christ. This communal aspect is highlighted in 1 Corinthians 12:13, "For in one Spirit we were all baptized into one body—Jews or Greeks, slaves or free—and all were made to drink of one Spirit." Baptism thus acts as a unifying practice, bringing together individuals from diverse backgrounds into a single faith community.

Theologically, baptism is interpreted as an outward sign of an inward grace. It is a visible symbol of the invisible work of the Holy Spirit in a believer's life. The water used in baptism is not merely a physical element but a conduit through which God's grace is imparted to the individual. This understanding is reflected in Titus 3:5, "He saved us, not because of righteous things we had done, but because of his mercy. He saved us through the washing of rebirth and renewal by the Holy Spirit."

In summary, the meaning of baptism is rich and multi-dimensional. It signifies cleansing from sin, spiritual rebirth, and initiation into the Christian community. Biblical references and theological interpretations together provide a comprehensive understanding of baptism's profound significance in the life of a believer. Through this sacrament, Christians experience a transformative act of faith, embodying their commitment to Christ and their integration into His church.

The purpose of baptism is deeply rooted in its spiritual significance, serving as a public declaration of faith and marking the entry into the Christian community. These intertwined purposes highlight baptism's vital role in the life of a believer and the broader church.

Spiritually, baptism is a profound act of faith that signifies a believer's union with Christ. It is through baptism that Christians identify with the death, burial, and resurrection of Jesus. This symbolic act represents the death of the old self, enslaved by sin, and the rebirth of a new self, alive in Christ. Romans 6:3-4 articulates this beautifully: "Or don't you know that all of us who were baptized into Christ Jesus were baptized into his death? We were therefore buried with him through baptism into death in order that, just as Christ was raised from the dead through the glory of the Father, we too may live a new life." In this sense, baptism is not merely a ritual but a transformative spiritual experience that underscores the believer's salvation and ongoing sanctification.

Beyond its spiritual significance, baptism serves as a public declaration of faith. When individuals are baptized, they openly profess their commitment to follow Jesus Christ. This public act of obedience to Christ's command in Matthew 28:19, "Therefore go and make disciples of all nations, baptizing them in the name of the Father and of the Son and of the Holy Spirit," demonstrates their willingness to live according to His teachings. By being baptized, believers make a visible statement of their inner faith, declaring to their family, friends, and the broader community their allegiance to Christ. This public profession is an essential aspect of discipleship, as it reinforces the individual's commitment and serves as a testimony to others.

Baptism also marks the entry into the Christian community, the body of Christ. It is through baptism that believers are incorporated into the fellowship of the church, becoming members of a spiritual family. This communal aspect of baptism is emphasized in 1 Corinthians 12:13, "For we were all baptized by one Spirit so as to form one body—whether Jews or Gentiles, slave or free—and we were all given the one Spirit to drink." Baptism thus creates a bond among believers, uniting them in their shared faith and common purpose. This sense of belonging and mutual support is crucial for spiritual growth and accountability within the Christian life.

In summary, the purpose of baptism encompasses its profound spiritual significance, its role as a public declaration of faith, and its function as the entry into the Christian community. Each aspect of baptism reinforces the others, creating a holistic experience that transforms the believer's life and integrates them into the life of the church. Through baptism, Christians affirm their faith, commit to discipleship, and become part of a supportive and loving community dedicated to living out the teachings of Jesus Christ.

TRUE PRINCIPLES OF CHRISTIANITY BOOK TWO

The historical origins of baptism can be traced back to the Old Testament and Jewish traditions, and its significance is enriched through the practices of John the Baptist and the baptism of Jesus. This evolution culminated in the early Christian practices and the development of the sacrament, making baptism a cornerstone of the Christian faith.

In the Old Testament, the concept of ritual purification through water is evident. Various ceremonial washings, known as mikvah, were performed to cleanse individuals from impurities, symbolizing spiritual purification and renewal. These practices were an integral part of Jewish religious life, as seen in passages like Leviticus 15:13, which prescribes washing with water to achieve ritual purity. While these rites were not identical to Christian baptism, they laid the groundwork for understanding the symbolic use of water for purification and sanctification.

The ministry of John the Baptist marked a significant turning point in the practice of baptism. John's baptism was one of repentance for the forgiveness of sins, as described in Mark 1:4, "And so John the Baptist appeared in the wilderness, preaching a baptism of repentance for the forgiveness of sins." John's call for repentance and his use of water baptism to symbolize spiritual cleansing and renewal resonated deeply with the Jewish people, who were familiar with the concept of ritual purification. However, John's baptism introduced a new dimension by focusing on repentance and the preparation for the coming of the Messiah.

The baptism of Jesus by John in the Jordan River holds profound theological significance. Although Jesus was sinless, His baptism symbolized His identification with humanity's sinfulness and His role as the Lamb of God who takes away the sin of the world. Matthew 3:16-17 narrates this pivotal event: "As soon as Jesus was baptized, he went up out of the water. At that moment heaven was opened, and he saw the Spirit of God descending like a dove and alighting on him. And a voice from heaven said, 'This is my Son, whom I love; with him I am well pleased.'" Jesus' baptism not only affirmed His divine sonship but also established a model for Christian baptism, signifying the descent of the Holy Spirit and the divine approval of the act.

In the early Christian church, baptism quickly became an essential rite of initiation and faith. The early Christians continued the practice of baptism as taught by Jesus and the apostles. In Acts 2:38, Peter proclaims, "Repent and be baptized, every one of you, in the name of Jesus Christ for the forgiveness of your sins. And you will receive the gift of the Holy Spirit." This declaration underscores the importance of baptism as both a symbol of repentance and a means of receiving the Holy Spirit. The early Christians baptized new converts in the name of the Father, Son, and Holy Spirit, following the Great Commission given by Jesus in Matthew 28:19.

As the early church grew, so did the understanding and practice of baptism. By the second and third centuries, detailed catechetical instruction and preparation periods, such as the catechumenate, were established for baptismal candidates. The sacrament became a more formalized and communal celebration, often conducted during significant liturgical seasons like Easter. This development reflected the growing recognition of baptism's profound theological and ecclesial significance.

In conclusion, the historical origins of baptism reveal a rich tapestry of religious and theological developments. From the ritual purifications of the Old Testament and Jewish traditions to the transformative ministry of John the Baptist and the baptism of Jesus, and finally to the early Christian practices and the formalization of the sacrament, baptism has evolved into a central rite of the Christian faith. It symbolizes repentance, purification, and initiation into the body of Christ, embodying the spiritual journey of believers through the ages.

Baptism plays a crucial role in the Christian life, signifying spiritual transformation and growth, embodying the symbolism of death and resurrection with Christ, and marking the beginning of an ongoing commitment to discipleship. Each of these elements interweaves to highlight the profound impact of baptism on a believer's journey of faith.

The act of baptism initiates a significant spiritual transformation. Through this sacrament, individuals undergo a profound inner change as they accept Christ and receive the Holy Spirit. This transformation is not merely symbolic but a real and powerful renewal of the heart and mind. As described in 2 Corinthians 5:17, "Therefore, if anyone is in Christ, the new creation has come: The old has gone, the new is here!" Baptism marks the beginning of a new life in Christ, characterized by a departure from the old, sinful ways and a step into a life led by the Spirit. This new life involves a continual process of spiritual growth, where the baptized believer seeks to deepen their relationship with God, grow in faith, and cultivate the fruits of the Spirit.

Central to the meaning of baptism is its symbolism of death and resurrection with Christ. In Romans 6:3-4, Paul explains, "Or don't you know that all of us who were baptized into Christ Jesus were baptized into his death? We were therefore buried with him through baptism into death in order that, just as Christ was raised from the dead through the glory of the Father, we too may live a new life." This imagery powerfully conveys that through baptism, believers participate in the death of Jesus, symbolically dying to their old selves and sinful nature. Emerging from the waters of baptism represents resurrection with Christ, rising to a new, transformed life. This identification with Christ's death and resurrection is foundational to the Christian experience, reminding believers of their redemption and the hope of eternal life.

Baptism also signifies an ongoing commitment to discipleship. It is not an end but a beginning, a pledge to live a life devoted to following Jesus and growing in faith. This commitment involves continual learning, obedience to God's Word, and participation in the life of the church. In Matthew 28:19-20, Jesus commissions His followers to "make disciples of all nations, baptizing them in the name of the Father and of the Son and of the Holy Spirit, and teaching them to obey everything I have commanded you." Baptism thus initiates a lifelong journey of discipleship, where believers are called to emulate Christ's example, engage in spiritual disciplines, and serve others in love.

Moreover, baptism connects believers to the broader Christian community, providing a support system for their spiritual journey. Being part of the church, the body of Christ, offers fellowship, accountability, and opportunities for service and growth. This communal aspect is essential for nurturing the faith and sustaining the commitment made at baptism.

In conclusion, baptism's role in the Christian life is multifaceted and deeply transformative. It signifies a profound spiritual transformation and growth, embodies the powerful symbolism of death and resurrection with Christ, and marks the beginning of an ongoing commitment to discipleship. Through baptism, believers embark on a journey of faith that continually draws them closer to God, integrates them into the Christian community, and inspires them to live out the teachings of Jesus in every aspect of their lives.

The Seventh-day Adventist understanding and practice of baptism are deeply rooted in theological foundations, emphasizing the significance of this sacrament as a declaration of faith, a symbol of spiritual rebirth, and a commitment to a life of discipleship. The process and prerequisites for baptism in the Adventist Church reflect a careful preparation that ensures a meaningful and informed decision by the candidates.

The theological foundation of baptism in the Seventh-day Adventist Church is built on the belief that baptism is a public declaration of an individual's faith in Jesus Christ and acceptance of His salvation. It signifies the washing away of sins, spiritual renewal, and entry into the body of Christ. This understanding aligns with biblical teachings such as Acts 2:38, which calls for repentance and baptism in the name of Jesus Christ for the forgiveness of sins. Additionally, Adventists view baptism as an outward sign of an inward change, representing the transformative power of the Holy Spirit in the believer's life, as described in Romans 6:3-4, where Paul speaks of being baptized into Christ's death and rising to walk in newness of life.

The process and prerequisites for baptism in the Seventh-day Adventist Church involve several steps to ensure that candidates fully understand the commitment they are making. Typically, individuals seeking baptism undergo a period of instruction, often through Bible studies or baptismal classes, where they learn about fundamental Christian beliefs, the teachings of Jesus, and the distinctive doctrines of the Adventist faith. This preparation period helps candidates develop a personal relationship with Christ and a clear understanding of the significance of baptism. Once the candidates have completed their preparation and expressed a sincere desire to follow Christ, they are baptized by full immersion, following the example of Jesus' baptism in the Jordan River. Full immersion is seen as the most accurate representation of the death, burial, and resurrection of Jesus, symbolizing the complete cleansing from sin and the start of a new life.

In comparison to other Christian denominations, the Seventh-day Adventist practice of baptism shares similarities and differences. Like many Protestant denominations, Adventists emphasize believer's baptism, meaning that individuals are baptized when they are old enough to make a personal decision to follow Christ. This contrasts with denominations that practice infant baptism, such as the Roman Catholic, Orthodox, and some Protestant churches, where baptism is administered to infants as a sacrament of initiation into the faith community. Additionally, the Adventist Church practices baptism by full immersion, similar to Baptists and Pentecostals, whereas some denominations, like the Lutheran and Methodist churches, may practice sprinkling or pouring as valid forms of baptism.

Personal testimonies and experiences of baptized members highlight the profound impact of this sacrament on their spiritual journeys. Many Adventists recount their baptism as a pivotal moment of commitment and transformation. For instance, one member might describe how their baptism marked the culmination of a period of intense spiritual searching and study, leading to a deep sense of peace and purpose in their newfound relationship with Christ. Another might share how the public declaration of faith during their baptism service strengthened their resolve to live according to biblical principles and fostered a stronger sense of belonging within the church community. These personal stories reflect the joy, renewal, and sense of responsibility that accompany the decision to be baptized, illustrating how this sacrament continues to inspire and transform lives within the Adventist Church.

In conclusion, the Seventh-day Adventist understanding and practice of baptism are grounded in theological foundations that emphasize its significance as a declaration of faith, spiritual rebirth, and commitment to discipleship. The process and prerequisites ensure that candidates are well-prepared and understand the profound meaning of their decision. While sharing similarities with other Christian denominations, the Adventist practice of full immersion and believer's baptism distinguishes it within the broader Christian context. Personal testimonies from baptized members highlight the transformative power of this sacrament, underscoring its vital role in the spiritual life of the Adventist community.

Baptism stands as a cornerstone of the Christian faith, embodying profound spiritual significance, personal transformation, and communal belonging. Throughout this chapter, we have explored the multifaceted nature of baptism, delving into its rich symbolism, historical origins, theological foundations, and contemporary practices. This sacrament, which has been practiced since the time of

Christ and continues to be a central rite in Christian life, holds deep meaning for believers.

At its core, baptism represents a powerful act of faith, signifying the washing away of sins, spiritual rebirth, and initiation into the body of Christ. It is a public declaration of an individual's commitment to follow Jesus and an outward expression of an inward change. The act of being baptized, particularly by full immersion as practiced by many denominations, vividly symbolizes the believer's identification with the death, burial, and resurrection of Christ, marking the beginning of a new life in Him.

The personal impact of baptism is profound. For each believer, it marks a pivotal moment of transformation and renewal. Through baptism, individuals experience a deep sense of spiritual cleansing and the empowerment of the Holy Spirit. It serves as a milestone in their faith journey, reminding them of their commitment to live according to Christ's teachings and to grow continually in their relationship with God. Personal testimonies of baptized members often reflect the joy, peace, and sense of purpose that accompany this sacred act.

Communally, baptism unites believers into the fellowship of the church, creating a sense of belonging and shared faith. It is a sacrament that not only transforms individuals but also strengthens the community of believers. Through baptism, Christians are welcomed into a spiritual family, where they find support, accountability, and opportunities for service. This communal aspect of baptism fosters a deep sense of connection and unity within the body of Christ, encouraging believers to support one another in their spiritual journeys.

As we reflect on the importance and meaning of baptism, it becomes clear that this sacrament is more than a mere ritual; it is a profound encounter with God's grace and a declaration of faith that shapes the entire Christian life. Baptism calls believers to a life of ongoing discipleship, where they continually seek to grow in faith, follow Christ's example, and engage in the life of the church.

In closing, I encourage you, dear readers, to contemplate your own spiritual journey. Whether you have already been baptized or are considering taking this step, reflect on the significance of baptism in your life. Consider how this sacrament can deepen your relationship with God, renew your commitment to follow Jesus, and integrate you into the loving and supportive community of believers. May the exploration of baptism inspire you to embrace its profound meaning and transformative power, guiding you on your path of faith and discipleship.

For those seeking to deepen their understanding of baptism, there are numerous resources available that provide theological insights, historical perspectives, and practical guidance. These resources include recommended readings, Bible study guides, and church materials that can enhance your knowledge and appreciation of this significant Christian sacrament.

One highly recommended book is "Believer's Baptism: Sign of the New Covenant in Christ" edited by Thomas R. Schreiner and Shawn D. Wright. This text offers a comprehensive theological exploration of baptism, examining its biblical foundations and significance within the context of the New Covenant. It provides valuable insights into the meaning and practice of baptism from a scholarly yet accessible perspective.

Another essential read is "Baptism: Three Views" by David F. Wright, Sinclair B. Ferguson, and Bruce A. Ware. This book presents different theological perspectives on baptism, including infant baptism, believer's baptism, and a mediating position. By exploring these differing views, readers can gain a well-rounded understanding of the theological debates and historical practices related to baptism.

For a historical perspective, "The History of Christian Baptism" by Robert Robinson is an excellent resource. This book delves into the

TRUE PRINCIPLES OF CHRISTIANITY BOOK TWO

development and practice of baptism throughout Christian history, tracing its origins from the early church to contemporary times. It provides a thorough examination of how baptism has evolved and its significance in various Christian traditions.

In terms of Bible study guides, "Baptism: A Bible Study Wordbook for Kids" by Richard E. Todd is an engaging resource for younger readers. It explains the meaning and importance of baptism in an age-appropriate manner, making it a valuable tool for parents and educators seeking to teach children about this sacrament.

For adults, "Baptism: A Study of Christian Baptism" by Jack Cottrell is a detailed Bible study guide that explores the biblical texts and theological concepts related to baptism. It is designed to help individuals and study groups delve deeply into the scriptural basis and significance of baptism.

Church resources can also be invaluable for those preparing for baptism or seeking to understand its role within a specific denomination. The Seventh-day Adventist Church, for instance, offers comprehensive materials for baptismal candidates. The "Seventh-day Adventist Church Manual" provides an overview of the church's teachings on baptism, including its theological foundations and practical guidelines. Additionally, the Adventist publication "Steps to Christ" by Ellen G. White is a highly recommended read for new believers. It offers spiritual guidance and insights into the Christian journey, making it an excellent companion for those preparing for baptism.

For a more interactive approach, many churches offer baptismal classes or Bible study groups specifically focused on this sacrament. These classes often include discussions on the theological significance of baptism, practical preparations, and personal testimonies. Participating in such classes can provide a supportive environment for individuals to explore their faith and prepare for baptism.

2. Understanding The Lord's Supper

The Lord's Supper, also known as Communion or the Eucharist, holds a place of profound significance in Christian practice. It is a sacred ritual that commemorates the Last Supper Jesus shared with His disciples before His crucifixion. This observance serves as a tangible expression of faith, a powerful act of remembrance, and a proclamation of the foundational truths of Christianity. By participating in the Lord's Supper, believers engage in a deeply spiritual experience that connects them to the life, death, and resurrection of Jesus Christ.

Historically, the practice of the Lord's Supper dates back to the early Christian community. The earliest accounts of this observance are found in the New Testament, particularly in the Gospels and the writings of the Apostle Paul. On the night before His crucifixion, Jesus gathered His disciples for a final meal, during which He instituted this ritual. He broke bread and shared wine, instructing His followers to do the same in remembrance of Him. This moment is captured in passages such as Matthew 26:26-29, Mark 14:22-25, Luke 22:14-20, and 1 Corinthians 11:23-26.

Theologically, the Lord's Supper is rich with meaning. It serves as a reminder of Jesus' sacrifice, where His body was broken and His blood was shed for the forgiveness of sins. This act of sharing bread and wine symbolizes the new covenant between God and humanity, sealed by Christ's sacrifice. The bread represents Jesus' body, which was given for believers, and the wine represents His blood, poured out for the remission of sins. This ritual not only commemorates Jesus' death but also proclaims His resurrection and the promise of His return.

Moreover, the Lord's Supper embodies the unity of the Christian community. As believers partake in the bread and wine, they do so together, symbolizing their oneness in Christ. This act of communal participation reinforces the bond among members of the church, reminding them of their shared faith and mission. It is a declaration of their collective identity as the body of Christ, united by His love and sacrifice.

Throughout history, the Lord's Supper has been a central element of Christian worship. It is observed in various forms across different denominations, each bringing its own theological emphasis and liturgical practice. Despite these differences, the core significance of the Lord's Supper remains consistent: it is a sacred commemoration of Jesus' sacrificial love and a celebration of the new life and unity that believers have in Him.

In essence, the Lord's Supper is more than just a ritual; it is a profound encounter with the divine. It invites believers to reflect on the depths of God's love, to remember the cost of their redemption, and to reaffirm their commitment to live in accordance with the teachings of Christ. As they gather around the table, they are reminded of the hope that lies at the heart of their faith—the promise of eternal life through Jesus Christ.

The Lord's Supper, a central rite in Christian worship, carries deep spiritual and symbolic significance. It is a practice rooted in the final meal Jesus shared with His disciples before His crucifixion, commonly referred to as the Last Supper. During this meal, Jesus instituted a ritual that would serve as a perpetual reminder of His sacrifice and a proclamation of the new covenant between God and humanity.

The origins of the Lord's Supper are found in the New Testament accounts of the Last Supper, documented in the Gospels of Matthew, Mark, and Luke, as well as in Paul's first letter to the Corinthians. On the night before His betrayal and arrest, Jesus took bread, gave thanks, broke it, and gave it to His disciples, saying, "This is my body given for you; do this in remembrance of me" (Luke 22:19). He then took a cup of wine, stating, "This cup is the new covenant in my blood, which is poured out for you" (Luke 22:20). These actions and words established a new ordinance for His followers, instructing them to repeat this meal in remembrance of Him.

The scriptural basis for the Lord's Supper is further reinforced in 1 Corinthians 11:23-26, where Paul recounts the events of the Last Supper and emphasizes its importance for the Christian community. Paul writes, "For whenever you eat this bread and drink this cup, you proclaim the Lord's death until he comes" (1 Corinthians 11:26). This passage highlights the dual purpose of the Lord's Supper: it is both a commemoration of Jesus' sacrificial death and a forward-looking anticipation of His return.

The terminology used to describe this practice varies across Christian traditions, reflecting different theological emphases and liturgical practices. The term "Eucharist" is derived from the Greek word "eucharistia," meaning "thanksgiving." It emphasizes the act of giving thanks for Christ's sacrifice and the blessings received through His death and resurrection. "Communion" is another common term, which underscores the communal aspect of the ritual—believers share in the body and blood of Christ and, through this act, experience a profound sense of unity with one another and with God. "The Lord's Supper" directly references the meal Jesus shared with His disciples, highlighting its origins and the instructions He gave to continue the practice in His memory.

Despite these differences in terminology, the essence of the Lord's Supper remains consistent across Christian denominations. It is a sacred act of remembrance and thanksgiving, a proclamation of faith in Jesus' atoning sacrifice, and a celebration of the new covenant established through His blood. By participating in the Lord's Supper, believers acknowledge their dependence on Christ for salvation, affirm their unity as members of His body, and look forward with hope to His promised return.

The Lord's Supper is a multifaceted practice that holds deep theological and spiritual significance. It is a tangible reminder of Jesus' love and sacrifice, a means of grace through which believers receive spiritual nourishment, and a powerful expression of the unity and hope that define the Christian faith. Through this sacred meal, Christians are drawn closer to their Savior and to one another, strengthened in their faith, and renewed in their commitment to live according to the teachings of Christ.

The Lord's Supper, deeply rooted in Christian tradition and practice, is a rich and profound ritual that carries multiple layers of significance. At its core, it serves as a commemoration of Jesus' sacrificial death. When believers partake in the bread and wine, they are reminded of the immense love and sacrifice of Jesus Christ, who gave His body and shed His blood for the salvation of humanity. This act of commemoration is central to the Christian faith, as it continually brings to mind the pivotal event of Jesus' crucifixion, which is the foundation of redemption and reconciliation with God.

The Lord's Supper is also an act of remembrance and proclamation. As Jesus instructed His disciples to do this in remembrance of Him, the ritual serves as a perpetual reminder of His sacrifice. Each time the bread is broken and the wine is poured, it proclaims the story of Jesus' death and the new covenant it established. This proclamation is not only a declaration of historical events but also an affirmation of the ongoing impact of Jesus' sacrifice in the lives of believers. It is a way to continuously tell the story of God's redemptive love and to acknowledge the transformative power of the cross.

Moreover, the Lord's Supper is an expression of unity among believers. When Christians gather to share in the bread and wine, they are participating in a communal act that transcends individual differences and unites them as one body in Christ. This unity is a profound aspect of the Lord's Supper, as it reflects the oneness of the church and the shared faith that binds its members together. The ritual emphasizes that, regardless of background or status, all believers are equal at the table of the Lord, symbolizing the inclusive nature of God's kingdom and the fellowship that is central to the Christian community.

Additionally, the Lord's Supper is a forward-looking anticipation of Christ's return. As Paul notes in 1 Corinthians 11:26, "For whenever you eat this bread and drink this cup, you proclaim the Lord's death until he comes." This aspect of the ritual instills hope and expectation within the hearts of believers. It is a reminder that Jesus' death is not the end of the story, but a part of the larger narrative that includes His resurrection and the promise of His return. By participating in the Lord's Supper, Christians reaffirm their belief in the eventual fulfillment of God's kingdom and the ultimate reunion with Christ.

In essence, the Lord's Supper encapsulates the heart of the Christian gospel. It commemorates Jesus' sacrificial death, serves as a powerful act of remembrance and proclamation, expresses the unity of the church, and anticipates the glorious return of Christ. Through this sacred meal, believers are drawn into a deeper relationship with their Savior and with one another, continually reminded of the love and grace that define their faith. The Lord's Supper is more than a ritual; it is a profound encounter with the divine, a celebration of the redemptive work of Christ, and a source of spiritual nourishment and hope for the Christian community.

The Lord's Supper employs specific emblems—bread, wine, and foot-washing—that carry profound symbolic meanings and theological significance. These elements are not only central to the ritual but also serve to deepen the understanding of Christ's sacrifice and the believer's relationship with Him and the Christian community.

The bread, a fundamental component of the Lord's Supper, is deeply symbolic. In Matthew 26:26, Jesus takes bread, blesses it, breaks it, and gives it to His disciples, saying, "Take and eat; this is my body." This act of breaking the bread represents Jesus' body, which was broken for the sake of humanity.

The bread symbolizes the physical suffering and sacrifice of Christ, who endured crucifixion to atone for the sins of the world. Theologically, the bread signifies nourishment, as it represents the sustenance provided by Jesus, the "bread of life" (John 6:35). It also symbolizes unity, as believers partake of the same bread, reflecting their shared participation in the body of Christ and their unity as members of His church.

The wine, another crucial emblem in the Lord's Supper, holds significant meaning. In Matthew 26:27-28, Jesus takes a cup of wine, gives thanks, and offers it to His disciples, saying, "Drink from it, all of you. This is my blood of the covenant, which is poured out for many for the forgiveness of sins." The wine symbolizes the blood of Christ, shed for the remission of sins. It represents the new covenant between God and humanity, established through Jesus' sacrificial death.

Theologically, the wine signifies purification, as it reflects the cleansing power of Christ's blood, which washes away sin and brings believers into a state of righteousness before God. It also symbolizes the covenant, the sacred agreement between God and His people, sealed by the blood of Jesus. This covenant assures believers of God's promises and their inclusion in His redemptive plan.

Foot-washing, although less universally practiced than the bread and wine, is another important element associated with the Lord's Supper. In John 13:1-17, Jesus washes His disciples' feet, setting an example of humility and service. He tells them, "Now that I, your Lord and Teacher, have washed your feet, you also should wash one another's feet" (John 13:14).

The act of foot-washing symbolizes humility, as it involves performing a task typically reserved for servants. It also represents service, demonstrating Jesus' teaching that greatness in His kingdom is measured by one's willingness to serve others. Furthermore, it signifies cleansing, as the washing of feet reflects the purification from sin and the readiness to walk in righteousness.

Theologically, foot-washing underscores the importance of preparation, as believers are called to prepare their hearts for service and worship. It also emphasizes equality, as Jesus, the Master, humbles Himself to serve His disciples, illustrating that all believers are equal in the sight of God. Finally, it fosters a sense of community, as the act of serving one another strengthens the bonds of fellowship and mutual care within the church.

In summary, the emblems of the Lord's Supper—bread, wine, and foot-washing—are rich with symbolic and theological significance. The bread represents the body of Christ, broken for believers, symbolizing nourishment and unity. The wine symbolizes the blood of Christ, shed for the forgiveness of sins, highlighting the themes of covenant and purification. Foot-washing embodies humility, service, and cleansing, emphasizing preparation, equality, and community. Through these emblems, the Lord's Supper invites believers to reflect deeply on the sacrifice of Jesus, their relationship with Him, and their commitment to live out His teachings in their lives and within their communities.

In the Christian context, an ordinance is a religious rite or practice that is observed as a commandment given by Jesus Christ to His followers. Ordinances are outward expressions of inward faith and obedience, serving as visible symbols of the grace and truth of the gospel. They are acts of worship and commitment that hold deep spiritual significance and are meant to be practiced regularly by believers as part of their faith journey.

One key distinction in Christian theology is between ordinances and sacraments. While both terms refer to religious practices, they carry different connotations and implications. Ordinances are typically understood as symbolic acts that do not convey grace in and of themselves but rather point to and remind believers of the grace already given through faith in Jesus Christ. They are seen as acts of obedience and commemoration, instituted by Christ and practiced by the church. Examples of ordinances include baptism and the Lord's Supper, both of which were commanded by Jesus and are observed in remembrance of His life, death, and resurrection.

Sacraments, on the other hand, are viewed in some Christian traditions, particularly within Catholic, Orthodox, and certain Protestant churches, as means by which God imparts grace to the participant. They are considered channels through which the Holy Spirit works to sanctify and strengthen believers. In these traditions, sacraments are more than symbolic; they are believed to have an intrinsic spiritual efficacy. For instance, in Catholicism, the Eucharist is seen as the actual body and blood of Christ, and baptism is believed to wash away original sin and bring about spiritual rebirth.

Despite these theological differences, the significance of observing these practices—whether termed ordinances or sacraments—remains profound across Christian denominations. These practices are essential for several reasons. Firstly, they are acts of obedience to Christ's commands. Jesus explicitly instructed His followers to baptize new disciples (Matthew 28:19) and to observe the Lord's Supper in remembrance of Him (Luke 22:19). By participating in these rites, believers demonstrate their submission to His authority and their commitment to living out His teachings.

Secondly, these practices serve as powerful reminders of key aspects of the Christian faith. Baptism symbolizes the believer's identification with Christ's death, burial, and resurrection, representing a public declaration of faith and a commitment to a new life in Christ. The Lord's Supper, with its bread and wine, vividly recalls Jesus' sacrificial death and the new covenant established through His blood. These tangible elements help to reinforce the central truths of the gospel and keep the focus of the church on the redemptive work of Christ.

Thirdly, the observance of these practices fosters a sense of community and unity among believers. Baptism often involves the public affirmation and support of the church community, welcoming the new believer into the fellowship of the faith. The Lord's Supper is typically celebrated together as a congregation, symbolizing the unity of the body of Christ and the shared faith of its members. These communal aspects of the ordinances help to build and strengthen the bonds within the Christian community, encouraging mutual support and accountability.

Finally, these practices provide opportunities for spiritual reflection and renewal. Participating in baptism and the Lord's Supper invites believers to examine their hearts, reflect on their relationship with God, and recommit to following Christ. They serve as regular reminders of God's grace and the transformative power of the gospel, prompting believers to live lives that honor and glorify Him.

In conclusion, ordinances in the Christian context are vital practices that encapsulate key elements of the faith. Whether viewed as symbolic acts of obedience or as means of grace, they hold deep significance for believers. By observing these practices, Christians not only obey Christ's commands but also engage in meaningful acts of remembrance, proclamation, unity, and spiritual renewal. Through baptism and the Lord's Supper, the church continually celebrates the redemptive work of Christ and strengthens the faith and fellowship of its members.

Preparing for the Lord's Supper, also known as Communion, involves both spiritual and practical aspects. This preparation ensures that the observance is conducted in a manner that honors the significance of the ritual and fosters a meaningful experience for all participants.

Spiritual preparation is crucial for both individuals and the congregation as a whole. The Apostle Paul emphasizes the importance of self-examination before partaking in the Lord's Supper. In 1

Corinthians 11:28-29, he writes, "Everyone ought to examine themselves before they eat of the bread and drink from the cup. For those who eat and drink without discerning the body of Christ eat and drink judgment on themselves." This self-examination involves reflecting on one's relationship with God, acknowledging any sins, and seeking forgiveness. It is a time for believers to repent, turning away from sinful behaviors and attitudes, and to reconcile with others.

Reconciliation is essential because the Lord's Supper symbolizes the unity of the body of Christ. Jesus taught that before offering a gift at the altar, one should first be reconciled with their brother or sister (Matthew 5:23-24). Thus, the period leading up to the Lord's Supper is a time for believers to mend broken relationships and seek peace with one another, ensuring that they approach the table with a pure heart.

Practical preparation is equally important to facilitate the smooth and reverent observance of the Lord's Supper. Setting up the service involves various logistical tasks, such as arranging the worship space, ensuring that the necessary items are in place, and creating an atmosphere conducive to worship. This includes preparing the emblems—typically bread and wine or grape juice. The bread is often prepared in a way that allows for easy distribution, such as being pre-cut or baked into small pieces. The wine or grape juice is usually poured into small cups or a communal chalice, depending on the tradition of the congregation.

The role of the clergy and the congregation in the preparation and observance of the Lord's Supper is integral. The clergy, often including pastors, priests, or elders, are responsible for leading the service and administering the sacraments. They guide the congregation through the liturgy, offering prayers, reading relevant scriptures, and delivering a message that highlights the significance of the Lord's Supper. Their leadership ensures that the observance is conducted with reverence and according to the doctrinal beliefs of the church.

The congregation also plays an active role in the preparation and observance. Members may assist in the practical setup, such as arranging the worship space and preparing the emblems. During the service, the congregation participates by receiving the bread and wine, joining in prayers and hymns, and engaging in moments of reflection and thanksgiving. The active involvement of the congregation underscores the communal nature of the Lord's Supper, as it is a collective act of worship and remembrance.

In summary, preparing for the Lord's Supper involves a balance of spiritual and practical preparations. Spiritual preparation includes self-examination, repentance, and reconciliation, ensuring that participants approach the table with a pure heart and a right relationship with God and one another. Practical preparation involves setting up the service, preparing the emblems, and ensuring that the logistical aspects are in place.

Both the clergy and the congregation have important roles in these preparations, contributing to a meaningful and reverent observance of the Lord's Supper. Through careful preparation, the church ensures that this sacred ritual is conducted in a manner that honors its profound significance and fosters a deep sense of unity and worship among believers.

The Lord's Supper, a profound and sacred tradition in Christianity, encapsulates the core of the Christian faith and its rich theological heritage. Throughout this chapter, we have explored its multifaceted significance, from its biblical origins and theological meanings to the symbolic emblems of bread, wine, and foot-washing. We have delved into the spiritual and practical preparations necessary for a meaningful observance, emphasizing the importance of self-examination, repentance, reconciliation, and the roles of both clergy and congregation.

At its heart, the Lord's Supper is a commemoration of Jesus Christ's sacrificial death, a poignant reminder of His body broken and His blood shed for the forgiveness of sins. This ritual is a powerful act of remembrance and proclamation, reaffirming the central truths of the gospel. It serves as an expression of unity among believers, symbolizing their shared faith and collective identity as the body of Christ. Furthermore, it looks forward with hope to the return of Christ, instilling a sense of anticipation and assurance of His promise to come again.

The ongoing relevance and importance of the Lord's Supper in Christian life and worship cannot be overstated. It remains a vital practice that connects believers to the historical events of Jesus' life and death, grounding their faith in the reality of His redemptive work. This ritual continually renews the commitment of believers to live out the teachings of Christ, fostering spiritual growth and strengthening the bonds of the Christian community. As a central element of worship, the Lord's Supper calls believers to reflect deeply on the significance of Jesus' sacrifice and to respond with lives characterized by gratitude, humility, and service.

In conclusion, the Lord's Supper is much more than a religious ritual; it is a profound encounter with the divine, a celebration of the redemptive work of Christ, and a source of spiritual nourishment and unity for the Christian community. It invites believers to engage in thoughtful and heartfelt participation, approaching the table with reverence and a deep sense of gratitude. By partaking in the bread and wine, Christians reaffirm their faith, remember the immense love and sacrifice of their Savior, and renew their commitment to follow Him. As you prepare to participate in the Lord's Supper, may you do so with a reflective heart, embracing the profound significance of this sacred meal and experiencing the deep spiritual communion it offers.

3. Empowered for Service

Spiritual gifts are special abilities bestowed by the Holy Spirit upon believers, enabling them to serve God and others in unique and effective ways. These gifts, which vary from individual to individual, are manifestations of the Spirit's power and presence in the life of a Christian. The Apostle Paul, in his letters to the early churches, particularly in 1 Corinthians 12, Romans 12, and Ephesians 4, emphasized the diversity and significance of these gifts, underscoring their divine origin and purpose.

The importance of spiritual gifts cannot be overstated. They are essential for the health and growth of the church, as well as for the fulfillment of God's mission in the world. Spiritual gifts equip believers to perform specific tasks that contribute to the common good, fostering unity and mutual edification within the Christian community. When exercised faithfully and humbly, these gifts not only build up the church but also glorify God, reflecting His grace and power in tangible ways.

The purpose of spiritual gifts in the Christian life is multifaceted. Firstly, they serve to edify and strengthen the church. Each gift, whether it is teaching, healing, prophecy, or administration, plays a crucial role in building up the body of Christ. By using their gifts, believers help one another grow in faith, knowledge, and maturity, creating a supportive and vibrant community of faith.

Secondly, spiritual gifts are instrumental in evangelism and outreach. They enable believers to effectively communicate the gospel, minister to those in need, and demonstrate the love and compassion of

Christ to the world. Whether through acts of service, words of wisdom, or miraculous signs, spiritual gifts make the message of the gospel more compelling and credible.

Lastly, spiritual gifts contribute to personal spiritual growth. As believers discover and exercise their gifts, they experience a deeper sense of purpose and fulfillment in their walk with God. They become more attuned to the leading of the Holy Spirit and more dependent on His power, which fosters spiritual maturity and a closer relationship with God.

In summary, spiritual gifts are divinely given abilities that empower believers to serve God and others effectively. They are vital for the edification of the church, the advancement of the gospel, and the personal growth of each Christian. Understanding and utilizing these gifts is essential for living a fruitful and impactful Christian life.

The concept of spiritual gifts is deeply rooted in Scripture, with several key passages providing a comprehensive understanding of their nature and purpose. Among these, 1 Corinthians 12, Romans 12, and Ephesians 4 are particularly significant, each offering unique insights into the diversity and function of spiritual gifts within the body of Christ.

In 1 Corinthians 12, the Apostle Paul addresses the church in Corinth, emphasizing the unity and diversity of spiritual gifts. He begins by affirming that all spiritual gifts originate from the same Spirit, highlighting that there are different kinds of gifts, but the same Spirit distributes them. Paul uses the metaphor of the body to illustrate how each gift, though different, is essential for the overall functioning of the church. Just as the body has many parts with different functions, so the church is composed of individuals with various gifts, each contributing to the common good. This passage underscores that spiritual gifts are given by the Holy Spirit for the purpose of building up the body of Christ and promoting unity among believers.

Romans 12 further expands on the theme of spiritual gifts, encouraging believers to use their gifts in service to one another. Paul exhorts the Roman Christians to offer their bodies as living sacrifices, which is their spiritual act of worship. He then lists various gifts, such as prophecy, serving, teaching, encouraging, giving, leading, and showing mercy, and urges believers to use these gifts according to the grace given to them. This passage emphasizes that spiritual gifts are acts of grace and should be exercised with humility, love, and a genuine desire to serve others.

Ephesians 4 provides another perspective on spiritual gifts, focusing on their role in equipping the church for ministry and fostering spiritual maturity. Paul explains that Christ gave gifts to His church, including apostles, prophets, evangelists, pastors, and teachers, to equip His people for works of service so that the body of Christ may be built up.

The goal is to attain unity in the faith and knowledge of the Son of God, becoming mature and attaining the whole measure of the fullness of Christ. This passage highlights that spiritual gifts are given not only for individual benefit but for the collective growth and maturity of the church, enabling believers to fulfill their calling and mission.

Central to the understanding of spiritual gifts is the role of the Holy Spirit in their distribution. The Holy Spirit is the source of all spiritual gifts, and He distributes them according to His will. This divine distribution ensures that the church has the necessary gifts to accomplish God's purposes. The Holy Spirit empowers believers, enabling them to perform tasks and ministries that they could not accomplish in their own strength. By relying on the Holy Spirit, believers can effectively use their gifts to serve God and others, demonstrating the power and presence of God in their lives.

In summary, the biblical basis for spiritual gifts is found in key passages such as 1 Corinthians 12, Romans 12, and Ephesians 4. These scriptures provide a comprehensive understanding of the nature, purpose, and function of spiritual gifts within the body of Christ. The Holy Spirit plays a crucial role in distributing these gifts, empowering believers to serve and build up the church. Through the faithful exercise of spiritual gifts, the church is strengthened, unified, and equipped to fulfill its mission in the world.

Spiritual gifts can be broadly categorized into three types: speaking gifts, service gifts, and power gifts. Each category encompasses a variety of specific gifts, each with its unique role and function within the body of Christ. Understanding these categories helps believers recognize the diversity of gifts and appreciate the different ways the Holy Spirit equips individuals for ministry.

Speaking gifts are those that involve communication and the sharing of God's truth. One of the prominent speaking gifts is prophecy. Prophecy involves receiving and conveying messages from God, providing guidance, encouragement, and sometimes correction to the church. Prophets play a vital role in communicating God's will and ensuring that the church remains aligned with His purposes. Teaching is another significant speaking gift.

Those with the gift of teaching have a unique ability to explain and interpret the Scriptures, helping others understand and apply God's word in their lives. Effective teachers play a crucial role in the discipleship and spiritual growth of believers. The gift of tongues is also a speaking gift. This gift involves speaking in languages that the speaker has not learned, which can be used for personal edification or, when interpreted, for the edification of the church. The gift of interpretation often accompanies tongues, allowing the message to be understood by the congregation. These speaking gifts are essential for communicating God's truth, encouraging the church, and promoting spiritual growth.

Service gifts are those that involve practical acts of service and support within the church community. The gift of helps is one such gift, where individuals have a special ability to assist others in practical ways, often behind the scenes. Those with this gift are invaluable in supporting various ministries and ensuring the smooth functioning of church activities. The gift of administration is another service gift. People with this gift excel in organizing, planning, and managing resources, helping to coordinate efforts and maintain order within the church.

This gift is crucial for effective ministry operations and long-term planning. The gift of mercy involves showing compassion and care to those in need, whether through acts of kindness, providing comfort, or offering support. Individuals with the gift of mercy are particularly attuned to the suffering of others and are driven to alleviate pain and hardship. These service gifts are vital for maintaining a healthy, functioning church community, where practical needs are met, and people are cared for and supported.

Power gifts are those that involve the manifestation of God's supernatural power. The gift of healing is a prominent power gift, where individuals are endowed with the ability to heal physical, emotional, or spiritual ailments through the power of the Holy Spirit. This gift serves as a powerful testimony to God's compassion and authority. Miracles are another power gift, involving extraordinary acts that go beyond natural explanation, demonstrating God's power in remarkable ways. These miracles can serve as signs that confirm the message of the gospel and inspire faith in believers and non-believers alike. The gift of faith is also considered a power gift. It involves a special endowment of trust in God's promises and His ability to act. Those with the gift of faith have an unwavering confidence in God's power and purposes, often inspiring others to trust God more deeply. These power gifts are instrumental in revealing God's supernatural presence and action, encouraging faith, and witnessing to the reality of God's kingdom.

In conclusion, spiritual gifts are diverse and multifaceted, encompassing speaking gifts, service gifts, and power gifts. Speaking gifts facilitate the communication of God's truth, service gifts ensure practical support and care within the church, and power gifts manifest

God's supernatural power. Each type of gift is essential for the health and growth of the church, enabling believers to fulfill their calling and contribute to the mission of the body of Christ. By recognizing and embracing these gifts, the church can operate effectively and harmoniously, reflecting the fullness of God's grace and power.

Discovering and understanding your spiritual gifts is a crucial step in fulfilling your God-given purpose and serving effectively within the body of Christ. This process involves self-assessment and prayer, seeking counsel from mature Christians, and taking practical steps to discern and confirm your spiritual gifts.

Self-assessment and prayer are foundational in identifying your spiritual gifts. Begin by reflecting on your passions, talents, and the ways God has used you in the past. Consider the activities and ministries that bring you joy and fulfillment, as these can often provide clues about your spiritual gifts. Prayer is essential in this process. Ask God to reveal the gifts He has bestowed upon you and to guide you in understanding how to use them. Through prayer, you can seek the Holy Spirit's wisdom and discernment, trusting that He will illuminate your path and help you recognize your unique contributions to the church.

Seeking counsel from mature Christians is another valuable step in identifying your spiritual gifts. Experienced believers can offer insights and perspectives that you might not have considered. Engage in conversations with pastors, mentors, and trusted friends who know you well and have observed your involvement in ministry. They can provide feedback on the strengths and abilities they see in you, helping you gain a clearer understanding of your gifts. Additionally, they can share their own experiences and guide you through the process of discerning and developing your gifts. The wisdom and encouragement of mature Christians are invaluable resources as you navigate this journey.

Practical steps to discern and confirm your spiritual gifts involve actively engaging in various ministries and observing where you are most effective and fulfilled. Start by volunteering in different areas of church life, from teaching and hospitality to administration and outreach. Pay attention to the activities that resonate with you and where you see positive impact and affirmation from others. Consider taking a spiritual gifts assessment, which can provide a structured way to evaluate your strengths and potential gifts. These assessments, often available online or through your church, can offer helpful insights and serve as a starting point for further exploration.

As you engage in ministry, be attentive to the feedback and responses from those you serve. Confirmation of your spiritual gifts often comes through the recognition and encouragement of others who witness your effectiveness in certain areas. If people consistently acknowledge your ability to teach, lead, show mercy, or administer, it is likely that you possess those gifts. Reflect on these affirmations and consider how they align with your personal sense of calling and fulfillment.

Moreover, be open to the Holy Spirit's leading and willing to step out in faith. Sometimes, spiritual gifts become evident only when we take bold steps to serve in new or challenging ways. Trust that the Holy Spirit will empower you and provide the necessary grace to fulfill your calling. As you grow in confidence and experience, your spiritual gifts will become more evident, and you will develop greater proficiency in using them.

In conclusion, identifying your spiritual gifts involves a combination of self-assessment and prayer, seeking counsel from mature Christians, and taking practical steps to discern and confirm your gifts. By engaging in this process with an open heart and a willingness to serve, you can discover the unique ways God has equipped you to contribute to the body of Christ. Embracing and utilizing your spiritual gifts will lead to a more fulfilling and impactful Christian life, benefiting both you and the wider church community.

The purpose and use of spiritual gifts are deeply intertwined with the core mission of the church and the personal growth of individual believers. Spiritual gifts are given by the Holy Spirit to fulfill specific functions that contribute to the overall health, unity, and effectiveness of the Christian community. They play a crucial role in the edification of the church, evangelism, outreach, and personal spiritual growth.

One of the primary purposes of spiritual gifts is the edification of the church. Each gift, whether it is teaching, prophecy, administration, or hospitality, serves to build up the body of Christ. Through the exercise of these gifts, believers can encourage, instruct, and support one another, fostering a sense of unity and mutual growth. For instance, the gift of teaching helps believers understand and apply God's Word, leading to deeper spiritual maturity.

The gift of prophecy can provide guidance and encouragement, aligning the church with God's will. Gifts like administration and helps ensure that the church operates smoothly, allowing other ministries to flourish. In essence, spiritual gifts are tools that God uses to nurture and strengthen His people, creating a vibrant and resilient community of faith.

Evangelism and outreach are also critical aspects of the purpose and use of spiritual gifts. Gifts such as evangelism, hospitality, and mercy enable believers to effectively share the gospel and demonstrate Christ's love to the world. Those with the gift of evangelism have a unique ability to communicate the message of salvation in compelling and relatable ways, drawing people to Christ. The gift of hospitality allows believers to create welcoming environments where non-believers can experience Christian love and fellowship. The gift of mercy empowers individuals to care for the hurting and marginalized, reflecting the compassion of Jesus. Through these gifts, the church can reach out to the broader community, meeting both spiritual and physical needs and making the gospel tangible and accessible.

Personal spiritual growth is another vital purpose of spiritual gifts. As believers discover and exercise their gifts, they experience a deeper sense of purpose and fulfillment in their relationship with God. The process of using spiritual gifts often involves stepping out in faith and relying on the Holy Spirit's empowerment, which fosters spiritual dependence and growth. For example, someone with the gift of teaching will grow in their understanding of Scripture and their ability to communicate it effectively as they prepare and deliver lessons. Similarly, a person with the gift of service will develop greater compassion and humility as they meet the needs of others. By using their gifts, believers not only contribute to the church and its mission but also grow in their own spiritual journey, becoming more like Christ in character and action.

In conclusion, the purpose and use of spiritual gifts encompass the edification of the church, evangelism, outreach, and personal spiritual growth. These gifts are divinely bestowed to ensure that the church is equipped to fulfill its mission, reach out to the world, and nurture the spiritual development of its members. Embracing and utilizing spiritual gifts allows believers to participate fully in God's work, building up the body of Christ and advancing His kingdom on earth.

Possessing spiritual gifts carries significant responsibilities for believers, requiring a heart of humility and service, an attitude that avoids pride and comparison, and a commitment to accountability and stewardship. These responsibilities ensure that spiritual gifts are used effectively and in a manner that honors God and benefits the church community.

Humility and service are foundational responsibilities for those with spiritual gifts. Believers must recognize that their gifts are not self-generated but are graciously given by the Holy Spirit for the purpose of serving others. This understanding should cultivate a sense of humility, as individuals acknowledge that their abilities and effectiveness in ministry are entirely dependent on God's power and grace. True humility manifests in a willingness to serve others selflessly, prioritizing the needs of the community over personal recognition or gain. For example, a person with the gift of teaching should approach their role with the mindset of a servant, eager to impart knowledge and understanding to others for their spiritual growth, rather than seeking personal acclaim. Similarly, those with gifts of helps or mercy should serve with compassion and kindness, reflecting Christ's love to those in need.

Avoiding pride and comparison is another critical responsibility for those with spiritual gifts. It is easy to fall into the trap of comparing oneself to others, either feeling superior because of one's gifts or inferior because of the gifts of others. Both attitudes are detrimental to the unity and health of the church.

Pride can lead to arrogance and a lack of cooperation, while feelings of inferiority can result in discouragement and disengagement. Believers must remember that all gifts are valuable and necessary for the body of Christ to function properly. As Paul writes in 1 Corinthians 12, the church is like a body with many parts, each with its own important role. No gift is more important than another, and all are needed for the church to thrive. By focusing on using their gifts to serve others rather than comparing themselves to others, believers can foster a spirit of unity and mutual respect within the church.

Accountability and stewardship are essential aspects of managing spiritual gifts responsibly. Believers are accountable to God for how they use the gifts He has entrusted to them. This accountability means that individuals should seek to use their gifts diligently and faithfully, not neglecting or misusing them. It involves being open to feedback and correction from others, recognizing that growth and improvement often come through the insights and guidance of fellow believers.

Stewardship of spiritual gifts also means being intentional about developing and honing these gifts. Just as a steward is responsible for managing resources wisely, believers are called to invest time and effort into nurturing their spiritual gifts, seeking opportunities for growth and training. This might include further study, practice, and seeking mentorship from more experienced individuals in the same areas of gifting.

In conclusion, those with spiritual gifts have the responsibility to approach their gifts with humility and a heart for service, avoiding pride and comparison, and committing to accountability and stewardship. By embracing these responsibilities, believers can ensure that their gifts are used in ways that glorify God, build up the church, and advance His kingdom. Spiritual gifts are not merely for personal benefit but are given to enrich the community and fulfill God's purposes. Properly managing these gifts leads to a thriving, united church where each member plays a vital role in the body of Christ.

While spiritual gifts are intended to build up the church and promote unity, they can also present challenges and opportunities for misuse if not properly understood and managed. Division and competition within the church, misunderstanding or neglecting gifts, and the need for corrective measures and healthy practices are key issues that need to be addressed to ensure that spiritual gifts fulfill their intended purpose.

One significant challenge is the potential for division and competition within the church. When individuals become overly focused on their own gifts or view certain gifts as more prestigious than others, it can lead to a sense of superiority or inferiority among believers. This can create an unhealthy environment of rivalry and comparison, where the unity of the church is compromised. For instance, those with more visible or public gifts, such as preaching or prophecy, might be tempted to feel more important than those with less visible gifts, like helps or mercy. Conversely, those with less visible gifts might feel undervalued or envious of others. Such attitudes can lead to factions and disunity within the church, undermining the purpose of spiritual gifts, which is to promote harmony and collective growth.

Another issue is the misunderstanding or neglecting of spiritual gifts. Some believers may be unaware of their spiritual gifts or unsure how to use them effectively. This can result from a lack of teaching and guidance on the topic within the church. Additionally, some may neglect their gifts due to fear, doubt, or a sense of inadequacy.

Others might misunderstand their gifts and attempt to use them inappropriately, without proper discernment or alignment with biblical principles. For example, the gift of prophecy, if not exercised with humility and a clear understanding of its purpose, can lead to misguided or harmful pronouncements that cause confusion or hurt within the congregation. Misunderstanding and neglecting gifts can lead to underutilization of the church's potential and hinder its mission.

To address these challenges, corrective measures and healthy practices are essential. Firstly, it is crucial to foster an environment of education and awareness about spiritual gifts. Churches should provide regular teaching and workshops to help members identify and understand their gifts. This includes offering spiritual gifts assessments and opportunities for individuals to explore different areas of ministry. Encouraging open dialogue about spiritual gifts can also help dispel misconceptions and promote a balanced view of all gifts.

Promoting a culture of humility and mutual respect is another vital corrective measure. Emphasizing that all gifts are valuable and necessary for the body of Christ can help counteract feelings of superiority or inferiority. Leaders should model and teach humility, encouraging believers to honor and appreciate the diverse gifts within the church. Recognizing and celebrating the contributions of all members, regardless of their gifts, fosters a sense of belonging and unity.

Accountability structures are also important for healthy use of spiritual gifts. Establishing mentorship and oversight can help individuals grow in their gifts while ensuring they are used appropriately. Experienced and mature believers can provide guidance, feedback, and correction when necessary, helping others develop their gifts in line with biblical principles. This can prevent misuse and promote a more effective and edifying exercise of spiritual gifts.

In conclusion, while spiritual gifts are intended to build up the church and promote unity, they can also present challenges such as division and competition, misunderstanding or neglecting gifts, and misuse. Addressing these issues requires corrective measures and healthy practices, including education, fostering humility and mutual respect, and establishing accountability structures. By doing so, the church can ensure that spiritual gifts are used effectively and harmoniously, fulfilling their purpose of edifying the body of Christ and advancing God's kingdom.

Developing and growing in your spiritual gifts is a lifelong journey that involves continuous learning and practice, seeking mentorship and discipleship, the importance of prayer, and a deep reliance on the Holy Spirit. Embracing these elements ensures that your gifts are used effectively and maturely, contributing to the growth and health of the church.

Continuous learning and practice are essential for the development of spiritual gifts. Just as natural talents require cultivation through study and application, spiritual gifts also need to be nurtured and refined. Engaging in regular study of the Scriptures, attending relevant workshops or seminars, and seeking opportunities to apply your gifts in various ministry contexts can greatly enhance your effectiveness. For example, if you have the gift of teaching, you can improve by studying educational techniques, theology, and different methods of biblical interpretation. If your gift is mercy, volunteering in environments where you can minister to the suffering will help you develop empathy and practical skills. Practice not only hones your abilities but also builds confidence and opens new avenues for service.

Mentorship and discipleship play a crucial role in the growth of your spiritual gifts. Having a mentor or being part of a discipleship relationship provides guidance, encouragement, and accountability. A mentor with experience in your area of gifting can offer valuable insights, help you navigate challenges, and encourage you to stretch beyond your comfort zone. For instance, a seasoned preacher can guide a novice in sermon preparation and delivery, providing constructive feedback and modeling effective communication.

Discipleship relationships also foster spiritual growth by encouraging you to emulate Christ and grow in your faith, which in turn enhances the use of your spiritual gifts. These relationships are vital for ongoing development and ensuring that your gifts are used in alignment with God's purposes.

The importance of prayer in developing spiritual gifts cannot be overstated. Prayer is the means through which we seek God's guidance, wisdom, and empowerment. Regularly praying for the Holy Spirit to reveal and cultivate your gifts keeps you attuned to His leading and dependent on His strength. Prayer also helps maintain a humble and servant-hearted attitude, recognizing that spiritual gifts are given by God for His glory and the edification of others. By continually seeking God's presence and direction in prayer, you align your heart with His will, ensuring that your gifts are exercised in a manner that honors Him and builds up the church.

Reliance on the Holy Spirit is foundational to the development and use of spiritual gifts. Spiritual gifts are supernatural endowments that require the Holy Spirit's empowerment to be effective. It is through His guidance and strength that we can truly minister in the power and love of Christ. Cultivating a close relationship with the Holy Spirit involves regular prayer, immersion in the Word of God, and a lifestyle of obedience and sensitivity to His prompting.

As you rely on the Holy Spirit, He will not only empower your gifts but also provide wisdom and discernment in their application. This reliance ensures that your ministry is not based on human effort or wisdom but on the dynamic and transformative power of God.

In conclusion, developing and growing in your spiritual gifts involves a commitment to continuous learning and practice, seeking mentorship and discipleship, the importance of prayer, and a deep reliance on the Holy Spirit. By embracing these elements, you can effectively nurture and enhance your spiritual gifts, ensuring they are used for the edification of the church and the glory of God. This process of growth and development is a lifelong journey, continually drawing you closer to God and enabling you to serve more effectively within His kingdom.

Ministries within the church are organized efforts and programs designed to serve various needs, promote spiritual growth, and advance the mission of the church. They encompass a wide range of activities and services that address the spiritual, physical, and emotional needs of both the church community and the broader society. Examples of various ministries include teaching and discipleship programs, worship and music ministries, outreach and evangelism efforts, pastoral care and counseling, children's and youth ministries, and service-oriented groups such as food pantries or homeless shelters. Each of these ministries plays a vital role in fulfilling the church's mission and vision, fostering a vibrant and active faith community.

Spiritual gifts significantly complement and enhance ministry work by equipping believers with the necessary abilities to serve effectively in different areas. For instance, someone with the gift of teaching may excel in leading Bible studies or adult education classes, providing deep and insightful instruction that helps others grow in their faith. Individuals with the gift of hospitality can create welcoming environments for newcomers, fostering a sense of belonging and community. Those with the gift of mercy may be drawn to pastoral care or counseling, offering compassion and support to those in distress. The gift of administration is crucial for organizing and managing church programs, ensuring that activities run smoothly and efficiently. By aligning spiritual gifts with ministry roles, the church can maximize its impact and ensure that each member is serving in a capacity that aligns with their God-given abilities and passions.

Encouraging participation and service within the church is essential for fostering a dynamic and engaged congregation. Leaders should actively identify and nurture the spiritual gifts of their members, helping individuals discover how they can contribute to the life of the church. This can be achieved through teaching about spiritual gifts, offering workshops or assessments to help members identify their gifts, and providing opportunities for people to serve in various ministries. Creating a culture of service where all contributions are valued and recognized encourages more people to get involved.

Church leaders can also set an example by demonstrating servant leadership and showing appreciation for the efforts of volunteers. Highlighting the importance of each ministry and how it contributes to the overall mission of the church can inspire members to take an active role. Providing training and support ensures that volunteers feel equipped and confident in their roles, which can enhance their effectiveness and satisfaction in serving.

Moreover, fostering a sense of community and teamwork within ministries helps build strong relationships and a supportive environment. When people feel connected and appreciated, they are more likely to stay engaged and committed to their ministry work. Celebrating successes, sharing stories of impact, and regularly communicating the vision and goals of each ministry can keep members motivated and focused on their purpose.

In conclusion, the role of ministries in the church is crucial for addressing the diverse needs of the congregation and community, promoting spiritual growth, and advancing the church's mission. Spiritual gifts play a vital role in enhancing ministry work, allowing believers to serve effectively and meaningfully. Encouraging participation and service within the church involves identifying and nurturing spiritual gifts, providing opportunities for involvement, and fostering a culture of appreciation and support. By doing so, the church can create a vibrant and active community where each member contributes to the collective mission and experiences the fulfillment of serving in their unique God-given capacity.

In conclusion, spiritual gifts and ministries are foundational aspects of the Christian life and the functioning of the church. Spiritual gifts, bestowed by the Holy Spirit, equip believers with unique abilities and strengths to edify the body of Christ, promote unity, and fulfill God's purposes. Ministries, organized efforts and programs within the church, provide avenues for believers to exercise their gifts in service to others, addressing diverse needs and advancing the mission of the church in the world.

Discovering and utilizing our spiritual gifts is not merely a personal endeavor but a vital component of our Christian discipleship. As each believer identifies and develops their gifts, they contribute to the health and vitality of the church community, ensuring that every member plays a meaningful role in the body of Christ. It is a call to action for believers to earnestly seek God's guidance through prayer, engage in self-reflection and assessment, and seek counsel from fellow believers to discern and affirm their spiritual gifts.

Furthermore, ongoing spiritual growth and service are integral to the faithful stewardship of our gifts. We are encouraged to continuously learn and practice, seeking mentorship and discipleship to refine our abilities and deepen our understanding of God's call on our lives. Through prayer and reliance on the Holy Spirit, we can navigate challenges, avoid pitfalls such as pride and comparison, and remain steadfast in our commitment to serving others with humility and love.

As we embrace our spiritual gifts and engage in ministries with diligence and passion, we embody Christ's example of servant leadership and sacrificial love. Let us encourage one another to step forward in faith, recognizing that each contribution, no matter how small, is significant in God's kingdom work. May our pursuit of spiritual gifts and faithful service be a testimony to God's grace and power, drawing others to experience His love and transforming presence.

In this journey of discovering, developing, and deploying our spiritual gifts, let us continue to grow in grace and knowledge, trusting that God who has called us will equip us abundantly for every good work. Together, let us press on towards the goal of glorifying God and building up His church, eagerly anticipating the day when we will see the fullness of His kingdom realized.

4. Insight, Revelation, and Discernment

The spiritual gift of prophecy is a profound and mysterious endowment bestowed by the Holy Spirit upon certain individuals within the Christian faith. To possess the gift of prophecy means to have the ability to receive and communicate messages from God. These messages, often referred to as revelations or divine insights, can include foretelling future events, offering guidance, providing warnings, or conveying God's will and purposes for His people. The gift of prophecy is not merely about predicting the future but is fundamentally about speaking forth God's truth and wisdom in a way that edifies, encourages, and comforts the church (1 Corinthians 14:3).

Understanding the spiritual gift of prophecy requires recognizing its purpose and role within the broader context of the Christian faith. Prophecy serves several key functions. It is a means by which God communicates directly with His people, offering guidance and direction for their lives. Prophetic messages can bring conviction of sin, leading to repentance and spiritual renewal. They can also provide encouragement and hope, particularly in times of trial and uncertainty. Moreover, prophecy plays a crucial role in building up the body of Christ, promoting unity, and fostering spiritual growth among believers. In this sense, the prophetic gift is a vital instrument for the church's spiritual health and vitality.

The biblical basis for the prophetic gift is deeply rooted in Scripture. From the earliest times, God has chosen prophets to be His spokespersons, delivering His messages to humanity. In the Old Testament, prophets like Isaiah, Jeremiah, and Ezekiel were pivotal figures who conveyed God's warnings, judgments, and promises to the people of Israel. Their writings form a significant part of the Hebrew Scriptures and continue to be revered as divine revelations.

In the New Testament, the prophetic gift is reaffirmed and expanded. The Apostle Paul, in his letters to the early Christian communities, emphasized the importance of prophecy as a spiritual gift. He encouraged believers to "eagerly desire gifts of the Spirit, especially prophecy" (1 Corinthians 14:1), highlighting its value in the church. Paul also provided practical instructions for the proper use of prophecy, stressing the need for order and discernment (1 Corinthians 14:29-33). The Book of Acts records instances of prophetic activity, such as the prophecies of Agabus (Acts 11:27-28; 21:10-11) and the daughters of Philip who prophesied (Acts 21:9), demonstrating that prophecy was an integral part of the early Christian experience.

The importance of prophecy in God's plan cannot be overstated. Throughout the Bible, prophetic messages have served as critical interventions in the unfolding narrative of God's relationship with humanity. They have provided divine direction, corrected moral and spiritual errors, and revealed God's purposes and plans for the future. In the context of salvation history, prophecy has pointed forward to the coming of Christ, the establishment of His kingdom, and the ultimate fulfillment of God's redemptive work. As such, prophecy remains a vital and dynamic aspect of the Christian faith, offering believers a powerful means of experiencing and understanding God's ongoing communication and activity in the world.

The prophetic gift is a central theme in the Bible, manifested through the lives and ministries of numerous prophets, both in the Old Testament and the New Testament. These prophets served as God's messengers, delivering His words to His people, guiding them, and often calling them back to righteousness and faithfulness.

In the Old Testament, prophets were pivotal figures who spoke on behalf of God, addressing the spiritual, moral, and social issues of their time. The prophets are traditionally categorized into two groups: the major prophets and the minor prophets. The distinction between major and minor prophets is based on the length of their writings rather than their importance.

The major prophets include Isaiah, Jeremiah, Ezekiel, and Daniel. Isaiah's prophecies, for instance, are filled with messages of judgment against sin, but they also contain profound promises of hope and redemption. Isaiah foretold the coming of the Messiah, the suffering servant who would bring salvation to the world (Isaiah 53). Jeremiah, often called the "weeping prophet," warned of the impending destruction of Jerusalem due to the people's unfaithfulness but also conveyed God's promise of a new covenant (Jeremiah 31:31-34). Ezekiel's visions included vivid symbols and dramatic acts, emphasizing God's sovereignty and the need for repentance (Ezekiel 37:1-14). Daniel's prophecies encompassed both immediate historical events and future eschatological visions, offering a glimpse into God's ultimate plan for humanity (Daniel 7-12).

The minor prophets, such as Hosea, Joel, Amos, Obadiah, Jonah, Micah, Nahum, Habakkuk, Zephaniah, Haggai, Zechariah, and Malachi, also delivered powerful messages. Though their books are shorter, their impact is significant. Hosea's life and ministry, for example, symbolized God's enduring love and faithfulness despite Israel's infidelity (Hosea 3:1). Amos championed social justice, condemning the exploitation of the poor and calling for righteousness and justice to flow like a mighty stream (Amos 5:24). Malachi addressed the spiritual lethargy and moral decay of his time, pointing forward to the coming of Elijah before the great and dreadful day of the Lord (Malachi 4:5-6).

In the New Testament, the prophetic gift continued to play a vital role, particularly in the early church. Prophecy was one of the spiritual gifts bestowed by the Holy Spirit, meant to edify, exhort, and comfort believers (1 Corinthians 14:3). The New Testament prophets were integral to the foundation and growth of the early Christian communities, providing guidance and revelation from God.

One notable example of prophetic ministry in the New Testament is Agabus. In the Book of Acts, Agabus is depicted as a prophet who foretold a great famine that would spread over the entire Roman world (Acts 11:27-28). His prophecy led the disciples to take action, providing aid to those in need. Later, Agabus also prophesied about the Apostle Paul's imprisonment, warning him of the hardships he would face in Jerusalem (Acts 21:10-11). This prophetic insight prepared Paul for the challenges ahead and demonstrated the practical role of prophecy in the life of the church.

Another example is the daughters of Philip the evangelist, who are described as having the gift of prophecy (Acts 21:9). Their inclusion highlights that the prophetic gift was not limited to a select few but was distributed among various members of the early Christian community, including women.

The role of prophecy in the early church extended beyond foretelling future events. It included revealing God's will, providing instruction, and encouraging believers to remain faithful amidst persecution and trials. Prophecy served as a means of divine communication, strengthening the church's unity and mission.

In both the Old and New Testaments, the prophetic gift was a dynamic and essential aspect of God's interaction with His people. Prophets served as conduits for God's messages, addressing immediate concerns and pointing to future fulfillments. Their words, often challenging and convicting, were instrumental in shaping the faith and practice of God's people throughout history. As such, the prophetic gift remains a profound expression of God's ongoing desire to communicate with and guide His people.

As we approach the culmination of history, the role of prophecy takes on even greater significance. The Bible anticipates a surge in prophetic activity as we near the Second Coming of Christ, and understanding this increase is crucial for believers.

The Bible foretells an escalation of prophetic revelations in the end times. In the Book of Joel, God promises, "I will pour out my Spirit on all people. Your sons and daughters will prophesy, your old men will dream dreams, your young men will see visions" (Joel 2:28).

This prophecy was partially fulfilled at Pentecost, as recorded in the Book of Acts, when the Holy Spirit descended upon the disciples, enabling them to prophesy and speak in various tongues (Acts 2:1-4, 17-18). However, many theologians believe that the ultimate fulfillment of Joel's prophecy will occur in the last days, signaling an outpouring of divine revelations and insights as we draw closer to the end of the age.

The increasing prophetic activity is linked to the signs of the times and the fulfillment of biblical prophecies. Jesus Himself provided a detailed account of the signs that would precede His return. In the Olivet Discourse, He spoke of wars, famines, earthquakes, and other calamities as "the beginning of birth pains" (Matthew 24:6-8). He also warned of false prophets and false messiahs who would attempt to deceive even the elect (Matthew 24:24). These signs are meant to alert believers to the approaching end and to the need for spiritual vigilance and readiness.

Prophecy in the end times serves multiple purposes. It acts as a source of encouragement, warning, and guidance for believers. Encouragement comes from the assurance that God is in control and that He has a plan for the ultimate redemption of His people. Prophetic messages can provide hope and strength, reminding believers that despite the trials and tribulations of the present age, God's promises remain steadfast and true. The visions of the New Heaven and New Earth, as described in the Book of Revelation, offer a glimpse of the glorious future awaiting those who remain faithful (Revelation 21:1-4).

At the same time, prophecy serves as a warning. The warnings issued by the prophets of old regarding judgment and the need for repentance are echoed in the prophetic messages of the end times. The Book of Revelation is filled with warnings about the consequences of rejecting God and embracing sin. The imagery of the seven seals, trumpets, and bowls depict the severe judgments that will befall the earth and its inhabitants. These warnings are meant to prompt repentance and a return to God before it is too late.

Guidance is another critical aspect of end-time prophecy. The prophetic gift provides direction on how believers should live in anticipation of Christ's return. Jesus urged His followers to stay alert and be prepared, likening His coming to a thief in the night (Matthew 24:42-44). The Apostle Paul reiterated this call to vigilance, encouraging believers to live soberly and righteously, looking forward to the blessed hope and the glorious appearing of our great God and Savior, Jesus Christ (Titus 2:11-13). Prophetic messages often emphasize the importance of maintaining faith, pursuing holiness, and being actively engaged in the mission of the church.

For believers today, the prophetic gift remains a vital source of spiritual insight and motivation. It calls us to examine our lives, align ourselves with God's will, and remain steadfast in our faith. As we witness the unfolding of biblical prophecies and the signs of the times, we are reminded of the urgency of our mission and the need to be prepared for the Lord's return. The prophetic gift, therefore, is not just about foretelling future events but about transforming our present reality in light of God's ultimate plan. It challenges us to live with a sense of purpose, expectation, and devotion, knowing that the fulfillment of all things is at hand.

In a world filled with diverse voices claiming divine inspiration, discerning true prophets from false ones is crucial for believers. The Bible provides clear criteria for identifying true prophets, warning about the dangers of deception and the need for spiritual vigilance.

The primary criterion for a true prophet is alignment with Scripture. A true prophet's message will always be consistent with the teachings and principles found in the Bible. Deuteronomy 13:1-4 warns against prophets or dreamers who advocate following other gods, emphasizing that fidelity to God's commandments is the ultimate test. Isaiah 8:20 further reinforces this, declaring, "To the law and to the testimony! If they do not speak according to this word, they have no light of dawn." Therefore, any prophetic message that contradicts the revealed Word of God is to be rejected.

Another essential aspect of identifying true prophets is the fruit of their ministry. Jesus taught that we could recognize false prophets by their fruits, stating, "A good tree cannot bear bad fruit, and a bad tree cannot bear good fruit" (Matthew 7:18). The character and conduct of a prophet, along with the impact of their ministry, provide significant evidence of their authenticity. True prophets lead lives marked by integrity, humility, and righteousness. Their ministries result in spiritual growth, repentance, and a deeper understanding of God's will among the people they serve.

False prophets, on the other hand, exhibit characteristics that betray their true nature. Deception and false teachings are hallmarks of false prophets. They may perform signs and wonders to deceive, as warned by Jesus in Matthew 24:24. However, their teachings often lead people away from the truth of the Gospel, promoting doctrines that are contrary to biblical teaching. These individuals may seek personal gain, power, or recognition rather than the glory of God and the well-being of His people.

The consequences of following false prophets can be severe. Throughout the Bible, there are numerous examples of individuals and nations led astray by false prophets, resulting in spiritual decay, judgment, and destruction. Jeremiah confronted false prophets who assured the people of peace when disaster was imminent, leading to the fall of Jerusalem (Jeremiah 6:14; 14:13-15). In the New Testament,

Peter warned that false prophets and teachers would introduce destructive heresies, bringing swift destruction on themselves and their followers (2 Peter 2:1-2).

To navigate these challenges, believers are equipped with tools for discernment. Prayer and spiritual discernment are foundational. James 1:5 encourages believers to seek wisdom from God, who gives generously to all without finding fault. Through prayer, believers can ask for the Holy Spirit's guidance to discern truth from error. Spiritual discernment, a gift from the Holy Spirit, enables believers to distinguish between spirits and recognize the authenticity of prophetic messages (1 Corinthians 12:10).

Community and accountability also play a vital role in discernment. The early church practiced communal discernment, testing prophetic messages in the context of the faith community. Paul advised the Thessalonians, "Do not quench the Spirit. Do not treat prophecies with contempt but test them all; hold on to what is good, reject every kind of evil" (1 Thessalonians 5:19-22). Involving mature, spiritually discerning believers in the process of evaluating prophetic messages helps prevent individual biases and errors.

In conclusion, discerning true prophets from false ones is essential for maintaining the integrity of the Christian faith. By adhering to biblical criteria, examining the fruits of a prophet's ministry, and utilizing the tools of prayer, spiritual discernment, and community accountability, believers can navigate the complexities of prophetic messages. This discernment ensures that the prophetic gift continues to edify, guide, and strengthen the church in alignment with God's truth and purposes.

Ellen G. White is a central figure in the history of the Seventh-day Adventist Church, renowned for her prophetic ministry and significant contributions to the Adventist movement. Her life and work have left an indelible mark on the church and continue to influence its direction and mission.

TRUE PRINCIPLES OF CHRISTIANITY BOOK TWO

Ellen G. White was born Ellen Gould Harmon on November 26, 1827, in Gorham, Maine. Her early life was marked by hardship and poor health, which was further compounded by a severe accident at the age of nine that left her with lifelong health challenges. Despite these difficulties, Ellen demonstrated a deep spiritual sensitivity and a strong commitment to her faith from a young age.

In 1844, during a period of intense religious fervor known as the Millerite movement, Ellen Harmon experienced a profound spiritual calling. Following the Great Disappointment, when Christ did not return as expected, she had a vision that confirmed God's continued guidance for the Adventist believers. This vision, along with subsequent revelations, marked the beginning of her prophetic ministry. In 1846, she married James White, a fellow Millerite and devoted Adventist leader. Together, they played a crucial role in organizing and establishing the Seventh-day Adventist Church.

Ellen G. White's prophetic ministry spanned more than seventy years, during which she received approximately 2,000 visions and dreams. Her key messages and visions encompassed a wide range of topics, including health and education, the nature of Christ's ministry in the heavenly sanctuary, the importance of Sabbath observance, and the imminent return of Christ. One of her most influential works, "The Great Controversy," outlines the cosmic battle between good and evil and emphasizes the importance of faithfulness and perseverance.

White's writings and teachings significantly shaped the doctrine and practice of the Seventh-day Adventist Church. Her advocacy for health reform led to the establishment of a comprehensive health message, promoting a balanced diet, exercise, and abstinence from harmful substances. This emphasis on health and well-being has become a distinctive feature of Adventism. White also championed the cause of education, leading to the founding of numerous schools, colleges, and universities that continue to operate worldwide.

The impact of Ellen G. White on the Seventh-day Adventist Church is profound. Her visions and writings provided a theological framework and a sense of identity for the early Adventist believers. She played a pivotal role in the development of key doctrines, including the sanctuary doctrine and the investigative judgment. Her guidance helped shape the church's organizational structure, ensuring a strong foundation for its growth and mission.

Ellen G. White's legacy and relevance extend far beyond her lifetime. Her writings continue to be a source of inspiration and guidance for Adventists around the world. Her emphasis on holistic living, including physical, mental, and spiritual health, resonates with contemporary concerns about wellness and sustainable living. Her prophetic insights into education, social justice, and mission work remain pertinent to the church's ongoing efforts to address the needs of a diverse and changing world.

Despite her significant contributions, Ellen G. White has faced criticisms and affirmations. Some have questioned the authenticity of her prophetic gift, citing instances of alleged plagiarism and doctrinal disagreements. Critics argue that her writings should be subjected to the same scrutiny as any other historical religious text. However, many Adventists and scholars affirm the validity of her prophetic ministry, pointing to the transformative impact of her work and the enduring relevance of her messages.

In conclusion, Ellen G. White's life and prophetic ministry have had a lasting influence on the Seventh-day Adventist Church. Her visions, writings, and teachings provided a foundation for the church's beliefs and practices, guiding its development and mission. Her legacy continues to inspire and challenge Adventists to live faithfully, pursue holistic health, and engage in meaningful service to others. While her prophetic gift remains a subject of debate, the profound impact of her contributions is undeniable, securing her place as a pivotal figure in the history of Adventism.

The prophetic gift, as explored throughout this chapter, holds profound significance in the Christian faith. From its origins in the Bible through the ministries of the Old and New Testament prophets, to its anticipated increase as we approach the Second Coming of Christ, prophecy remains a vital means of divine communication. It serves to guide, warn, encourage, and edify believers, continually reminding them of God's ongoing involvement in human history.

In the past, prophets played a crucial role in conveying God's messages to His people. Figures like Isaiah, Jeremiah, and Ezekiel in the Old Testament, and Agabus and the daughters of Philip in the New Testament, exemplified the diverse and impactful nature of prophetic ministry. Their messages, rooted in divine revelation, called people to repentance, provided hope in times of despair, and pointed forward to God's redemptive plans.

In the present, the prophetic gift continues to be relevant. Believers are called to discern true prophetic messages by ensuring they align with Scripture and bear good spiritual fruit. The life and ministry of Ellen G. White illustrate how the prophetic gift can shape and guide a faith community, offering insights into health, education, and spirituality that resonate even today.

Looking to the future, prophecy will play an increasingly critical role as we near the Second Coming of Christ. The Bible predicts an upsurge in prophetic activity, providing guidance and warning to help believers remain vigilant. Prophetic messages will continue to prepare the faithful, encouraging them to stay true to their faith amidst the challenges and deceptions of the end times.

Believers are encouraged to embrace and discern the prophetic gift with wisdom and humility. Prayer, spiritual discernment, and community accountability are essential tools for navigating prophetic messages. By staying rooted in Scripture and seeking the Holy Spirit's guidance, believers can differentiate between true and false prophets, ensuring they follow God's genuine revelations.

Remaining vigilant and faithful is paramount as we anticipate the Second Coming. Prophetic messages serve as reminders of the urgency of our mission and the need for spiritual readiness. Believers are called to live with purpose, actively engaging in the work of the church, and maintaining a strong, personal relationship with God.

5. Origin, Commandments, and Purpose of Divine Law

God's Law, often referred to as the divine commandments or moral code, is a central tenet in Christianity that encompasses the rules and principles given by God to guide human conduct. Traditionally, this includes the Ten Commandments given to Moses on Mount Sinai, as well as other laws found throughout the Bible. These laws serve as a foundation for ethical behavior, spiritual devotion, and the overall relationship between humanity and the divine.

The importance of God's Law in Christianity cannot be overstated. It provides a moral compass for believers, delineating what is right and wrong according to divine standards. The Law serves several crucial functions.

First, it reveals the character of God, highlighting His holiness, justice, and love. By understanding and adhering to God's Law, Christians strive to reflect these divine attributes in their own lives. Second, the Law acts as a mirror, exposing human sinfulness and the need for repentance and redemption. It underscores the reality that all have sinned and fall short of the glory of God, thus pointing to the necessity of a Savior. Third, God's Law establishes a framework for a just and harmonious society, promoting values such as honesty, respect, and compassion.

The key themes within the discussion of God's Law in Christianity include its origins, its purpose, and its fulfillment in the New Testament. The origin of God's Law can be traced back to the Old Testament, where it was given to the Israelites as part of the covenant between God and His chosen people. This covenantal context emphasizes the relationship between obedience to the Law and the blessings of God's favor.

The purpose of God's Law extends beyond mere legalism; it is intended to guide believers into a deeper relationship with God and to foster community among His people. The Law teaches principles of justice, mercy, and faithfulness, urging believers to live lives that honor God and serve others. Furthermore, the New Testament brings a transformative perspective on God's Law, particularly through the teachings of Jesus Christ. Jesus affirmed the validity of the Law but also emphasized its fulfillment through love and grace. He taught that the greatest commandments are to love God with all one's heart, soul, and mind, and to love one's neighbor as oneself. In doing so, Jesus highlighted the essence of God's Law as relational and love-centered.

In summary, God's Law is a foundational aspect of Christianity, defining moral conduct, revealing divine attributes, and pointing to the need for redemption. Its themes of origin, purpose, and fulfillment through Christ provide a comprehensive understanding of its role and significance in the life of a believer. Through adherence to God's Law, Christians seek to live in a manner that reflects God's holiness and love, fostering a just and compassionate community.

The origin of God's Law is deeply rooted in the biblical narrative, tracing its foundations back to the earliest stories of humanity's relationship with the divine. The Biblical Foundations of God's Law begin with the creation story in Genesis, where God's command to Adam and Eve to refrain from eating the forbidden fruit establishes the concept of divine commandments. This narrative introduces the fundamental idea that God's instructions are intended to guide human behavior and maintain harmony between the Creator and His creation.

The Mosaic Law, given through Moses, is a pivotal moment in the development of God's Law. Central to the Mosaic Law are the Ten Commandments, which were delivered to the Israelites on Mount

Sinai. These commandments are concise, moral imperatives that outline fundamental principles for ethical living. They include directives to worship God alone, honor one's parents, refrain from murder, adultery, theft, false witness, and coveting. The Ten Commandments serve as a summary of God's moral expectations and are foundational to both Jewish and Christian ethical teachings.

Beyond the Ten Commandments, the Torah contains additional laws that expand on these basic principles. These laws cover various aspects of daily life, including dietary regulations, ceremonial practices, civil justice, and social welfare. They are detailed in books such as Leviticus, Numbers, and Deuteronomy and collectively form a comprehensive legal and ethical code for the Israelite community. The purpose of these laws was to set apart the Israelites as a holy people dedicated to God, providing guidelines for maintaining purity, justice, and communal harmony.

God's Covenants with Humanity are crucial to understanding the context and significance of His Law. The Abrahamic Covenant, established with Abraham, promised that his descendants would become a great nation through which all the families of the earth would be blessed. This covenantal relationship was marked by the practice of circumcision as a sign of belonging to God's chosen people. The Abrahamic Covenant underscores the idea that God's Law is given within the framework of a loving and purposeful relationship with His people.

The Mosaic Covenant, established with the Israelites at Mount Sinai, further elaborates on this relationship. In this covenant, God promises to be the God of Israel, and in return, the Israelites commit to obeying His Law. The Mosaic Covenant is characterized by the giving of the Law and the establishment of a sacrificial system to atone for sins. This covenant highlights the reciprocal nature of the relationship between God and His people, where obedience to the Law brings blessings and disobedience results in consequences.

FRANK M. CARAVEO

The Historical Context of God's Law is also significant, particularly in relation to Ancient Near Eastern legal traditions. The laws given to the Israelites were not created in a vacuum but were influenced by and responded to the legal norms of the surrounding cultures. Ancient Near Eastern societies, such as Babylon and Assyria, had their own codified laws, like the Code of Hammurabi, which dealt with similar issues of justice, property rights, and social order. However, God's Law for the Israelites was distinctive in its emphasis on the covenantal relationship with God and the ethical and moral dimensions that reflected His holiness and justice.

In Israelite society, the Law played a central role in shaping both religious and communal life. It was intended to govern not just individual behavior but also the collective life of the nation. The Law was read publicly, taught by priests and scribes, and was integral to the education and formation of the community. Festivals, sacrifices, and other religious practices were all regulated by the Law, ensuring that the worship and daily life of the Israelites were aligned with God's will.

In summary, the origin of God's Law is deeply embedded in the biblical narrative, beginning with the early commandments in Genesis and culminating in the comprehensive legal code given through Moses. The Ten Commandments and additional laws in the Torah provide a detailed framework for ethical and religious life. God's Covenants with Humanity, particularly the Abrahamic and Mosaic Covenants, underscore the relational and purposeful nature of these laws. The historical context of Ancient Near Eastern legal traditions and the central role of the Law in Israelite society further illuminate the unique and enduring significance of God's Law in guiding His people.

The Commandments in God's Law form the core of Christian ethics, providing a moral and spiritual framework for believers. At the heart of these commandments are the Ten Commandments, given to Moses on Mount Sinai. Each of these commandments carries profound significance for guiding Christian conduct and shaping the moral landscape of Christian communities.

The first commandment, "You shall have no other gods before me," emphasizes the exclusive worship of the one true God. This commandment underscores the principle of monotheism and demands loyalty and devotion to God above all else. In Christian ethics, this commandment is foundational, as it calls believers to prioritize their relationship with God and reject idolatry in all its forms.

The second commandment, "You shall not make for yourself an image," prohibits the creation and worship of idols. This reinforces the idea that God is spirit and cannot be represented by physical objects. In Christian practice, this commandment guards against the reduction of divine worship to mere rituals and emphasizes the importance of a genuine spiritual relationship with God.

The third commandment, "You shall not misuse the name of the Lord your God," calls for reverence in speaking about God. It forbids using God's name in vain or for dishonest purposes. This commandment highlights the sacredness of God's name and encourages believers to speak and act with integrity, reflecting their respect for God in all they do.

The fourth commandment, "Remember the Sabbath day by keeping it holy," instructs believers to set aside one day of the week for rest and worship. This commandment serves as a reminder of God's creation and His rest on the seventh day. In Christian ethics, the Sabbath is a time for rest, reflection, and renewal, fostering a deeper connection with God and community.

The fifth commandment, "Honor your father and your mother," emphasizes the importance of family relationships and respect for parental authority. This commandment promotes the values of obedience, care, and gratitude within the family unit, which is seen as a fundamental building block of a stable and harmonious society.

The sixth commandment, "You shall not murder," upholds the sanctity of human life. It forbids the taking of innocent life and calls for the protection and preservation of life. In Christian ethics, this commandment underlines the inherent value and dignity of every human being, created in the image of God.

The seventh commandment, "You shall not commit adultery," safeguards the sanctity of marriage and sexual integrity. It prohibits infidelity and promotes faithfulness within the marital relationship. This commandment underscores the importance of trust, commitment, and purity in personal relationships, reflecting the covenantal nature of marriage.

The eighth commandment, "You shall not steal," enjoins respect for the property and rights of others. It condemns theft and promotes honesty and fairness in all dealings. In Christian ethics, this commandment fosters a sense of justice and respect for the possessions and well-being of others.

The ninth commandment, "You shall not give false testimony against your neighbor," prohibits lying and bearing false witness. It calls for truthfulness and integrity in all communication. This commandment highlights the importance of honesty and the detrimental effects of deceit on personal and communal relationships.

The tenth commandment, "You shall not covet," addresses the inward attitudes of the heart, forbidding envy and covetousness. It encourages contentment and gratitude for what one has. In Christian ethics, this commandment reminds believers to guard against the destructive power of greed and to cultivate a spirit of thankfulness and generosity.

Beyond the Ten Commandments, other key commandments in God's Law can be categorized into moral, ceremonial, and civil laws. Moral laws encompass ethical principles that govern personal conduct and interpersonal relationships, such as laws against lying, stealing, and committing acts of violence. Ceremonial laws pertain to religious rituals, sacrifices, and purity practices that were specific to the worship practices of ancient Israel. Civil laws relate to the governance of society, including regulations on justice, property rights, and social responsibilities.

Jesus' Summary of the Law provides a profound encapsulation of these commandments. When asked about the greatest commandment, Jesus responded, "Love the Lord your God with all your heart and with all your soul and with all your mind." This greatest commandment encapsulates the essence of the first four commandments, emphasizing total devotion and love for God.

The second commandment, "Love your neighbor as yourself," summarizes the remaining six commandments, highlighting the importance of love, respect, and compassion in human relationships. These two commandments, according to Jesus, are the foundation upon which all the Law and the Prophets hang.

In conclusion, the Commandments in God's Law are essential to Christian ethics, providing clear directives for how believers should live in relation to God and others. The Ten Commandments offer a concise moral code, while other key commandments, including moral, ceremonial, and civil laws, offer further guidance. Jesus' summary of the Law with the greatest and second commandments underscores the centrality of love in fulfilling God's Law. Through adherence to these commandments, Christians seek to reflect God's character and live in harmony with His will.

The purpose of God's Law is multifaceted, encompassing profound theological, ethical, and redemptive dimensions. One of the primary purposes of God's Law is to reveal His character. Through the commandments and statutes, God's holiness, justice, and love are made evident. God's holiness is reflected in the Law's demand for moral purity and separation from sin. The commandments call for a lifestyle that mirrors God's own perfection and sets His people apart from the moral corruption of the world. In doing so, the Law underscores the transcendence and purity of God, calling believers to emulate His holiness in their daily lives.

The justice of God is also manifest in His Law. The commandments promote fairness, equity, and righteousness, reflecting God's just nature. Laws against theft, false witness, and murder protect the rights and dignity of individuals, while provisions for the poor, the stranger, and the marginalized reveal God's concern for social justice. The Law serves as a blueprint for a just society, where the vulnerable are protected, and the rights of all are upheld. This aspect of the Law reveals God's desire for a world where justice prevails and His people act with integrity and compassion.

God's love is perhaps most profoundly expressed through His Law. The commandments are given not as arbitrary rules but as expressions of God's loving care for His people. They are designed to lead to human flourishing and well-being. By following God's Law, believers experience the fullness of life that God intends for them. The call to love one's neighbor as oneself encapsulates the Law's emphasis on relational harmony and selfless concern for others, reflecting the boundless love of God.

God's Law also serves to guide moral conduct. It provides an ethical framework for living, offering clear instructions on what is right and wrong. The commandments address various aspects of human behavior, from personal integrity to social responsibilities, creating a comprehensive guide for ethical living. This framework helps believers navigate the complexities of life, making choices that align with God's will and promote the common good. The Law's guidance extends to social justice and community life, promoting values such as honesty, fidelity, and compassion, which are essential for a cohesive and just society.

Another crucial purpose of God's Law is to lead believers to Christ. In the New Testament, the Apostle Paul describes the Law as a tutor or guardian that leads us to Christ. The Law exposes human sinfulness by setting a standard that no one can perfectly uphold. This recognition of sin creates an awareness of the need for a Savior. The Law shows that despite human efforts, perfection is unattainable, and thus, it points to the necessity of grace and redemption found in Jesus Christ.

The role of the Law in recognizing sin is fundamental. It acts as a mirror, reflecting human shortcomings and revealing the pervasive nature of sin. By highlighting what is contrary to God's will, the Law makes individuals aware of their moral failings and their need for repentance. This recognition drives believers to seek forgiveness and transformation through Jesus, who perfectly fulfills the requirements of the Law.

The fulfillment of the Law through Jesus is a central theme in Christian theology. Jesus affirmed the Law's validity but also brought it to its full expression. He taught that He came not to abolish the Law but to fulfill it. In His life, death, and resurrection, Jesus embodies the perfect obedience to God's Law that humanity could not achieve. His sacrificial death atones for the sins that the Law exposes, and His resurrection opens the way for new life. Through faith in Jesus, believers receive the righteousness that comes from Him, fulfilling the Law's demands and entering into a restored relationship with God.

In summary, the purpose of God's Law is rich and varied. It reveals God's character, highlighting His holiness, justice, and love. It guides moral conduct, providing an ethical framework for personal and social living. It leads to Christ by exposing sin and pointing to the need for a Savior. Ultimately, the Law finds its fulfillment in Jesus, who perfectly embodies its principles and offers redemption to all who believe. Through the Law, believers are called to reflect God's character, live justly and lovingly, and find their ultimate hope and salvation in Christ.

The Law in the New Testament is understood through the lens of Jesus' teachings and the writings of the apostles, particularly Paul. This section explores how the Law is interpreted and applied within the New Testament, highlighting the continuity and transformation it undergoes in light of the life and teachings of Jesus Christ.

Jesus and the Law are intricately connected. In His ministry, Jesus affirmed the validity of the Law while also offering a deeper interpretation that emphasized its spiritual and ethical dimensions. Jesus' teachings on the Law often sought to go beyond mere legalistic observance, urging His followers to grasp the underlying principles of love, mercy, and justice. One of the clearest expositions of this approach is found in the Sermon on the Mount.

In the Sermon on the Mount, Jesus expounds on the true spirit of the Law. He begins by affirming, "Do not think that I have come to abolish the Law or the Prophets; I have not come to abolish them but to fulfill them." Here, Jesus clarifies that His mission is not to negate the Law but to bring it to its intended completion. He then provides a series of teachings that deepen and radicalize the understanding of the Law. For instance, while the Law prohibits murder, Jesus extends this prohibition to include anger and insults, highlighting the importance of reconciliation.

Similarly, He expands the commandment against adultery to encompass lustful thoughts, emphasizing purity of heart. Through these teachings, Jesus reveals that the Law is not merely about external compliance but about inner transformation and wholehearted devotion to God.

Paul and the Law present another critical aspect of the New Testament's understanding of God's commandments. Paul addresses the relationship between the Law and faith extensively in his letters. Central to his theology is the concept of justification by faith. Paul asserts that no one can be justified by the works of the Law, as all have sinned and fall short of God's glory. Instead, justification comes through faith in Jesus Christ. This does not mean that the Law is irrelevant; rather, Paul sees the Law as highlighting human sinfulness and pointing towards the need for a Savior. In this sense, the Law acts as a tutor that leads believers to Christ, where they find grace and redemption.

Paul also addresses the role of the Law in the life of a believer. While justification is by faith and not by works, the moral principles of the Law continue to be relevant. Paul emphasizes that believers are to live by the Spirit, which enables them to fulfill the righteous requirements of the Law. The ethical teachings of the Law, such as love, justice, and holiness, are still applicable, but they are now approached through the transformative power of the Holy Spirit rather than mere human effort.

The New Testament also explores the continuity and discontinuity of the Law. The Old Covenant, established through Moses, is marked by the giving of the Law at Mount Sinai and includes various ceremonial, civil, and moral laws. With the coming of Jesus, the New Covenant is inaugurated, fulfilling the promises of the Old Covenant and bringing about a new relationship between God and humanity. This New Covenant, prophesied in Jeremiah, emphasizes a transformed heart and an internalized Law written on the hearts of believers.

The relevance of the Law for Christians today is a topic of considerable importance. The moral principles of the Law, such as those found in the Ten Commandments, continue to provide a vital ethical framework. These commandments reflect God's character and His design for human flourishing. However, the ceremonial and civil aspects of the Law, which were specific to the cultural and religious context of ancient Israel, are seen as fulfilled and transformed in Christ. Practices such as animal sacrifices and dietary restrictions are no longer binding for Christians, as they were symbolic and preparatory, pointing towards the ultimate sacrifice of Jesus.

In summary, the Law in the New Testament is affirmed, deepened, and transformed through the life and teachings of Jesus. The Sermon on the Mount illustrates Jesus' approach to fulfilling the Law by emphasizing its spiritual and ethical dimensions. Paul elucidates the relationship between the Law and faith, emphasizing justification by faith and the ongoing moral relevance of the Law. The continuity and discontinuity of the Law are navigated through the distinction between the Old and New Covenants, with the New Covenant bringing a renewed understanding and internalization of God's commandments. For Christians today, the Law remains a crucial guide for ethical living, rooted in the love and grace of Jesus Christ, who fulfills and transcends the ancient legal code.

The practical application of God's Law is a vital aspect of Christian living, translating theological principles into everyday actions. Central to this is the concept of living by the Spirit, which empowers believers to embody the ethical and moral teachings of the Law in their lives. Living by the Spirit involves a dynamic relationship with the Holy Spirit, who indwells believers and guides them in aligning their lives with God's will. This divine empowerment enables Christians to overcome the limitations of human effort and live in a way that reflects God's holiness and love.

The Fruit of the Spirit, as outlined in Galatians, represents the visible outcomes of a life led by the Holy Spirit. These include love, joy, peace, patience, kindness, goodness, faithfulness, gentleness, and self-control. These attributes reflect the character of Christ and serve as practical manifestations of God's Law in action. By cultivating the Fruit of the Spirit, believers demonstrate the transformative power of God's grace in their lives, showing how the ethical demands of the Law can be met through the Spirit's work.

Empowerment for holy living is a key aspect of applying God's Law practically. The Holy Spirit provides the strength and guidance needed to pursue a life of holiness. This includes not only avoiding sin but also actively pursuing righteousness and good works. The empowerment of the Spirit allows believers to fulfill the deeper ethical demands of the

Law, such as loving their neighbors and seeking justice, beyond mere external compliance.

Ethical decision-making is another crucial area where God's Law finds practical application. Christians are called to apply the principles of the Law to contemporary issues, navigating the complexities of modern life with biblical wisdom. This involves discerning God's will in situations that may not be explicitly addressed in Scripture but require a moral and ethical response. By grounding their decisions in the teachings of the Law and the guidance of the Holy Spirit, believers can make choices that honor God and promote the common good.

The role of the Church in moral guidance is also significant. As the community of believers, the Church provides a context for teaching and applying God's Law. Through preaching, teaching, and pastoral care, the Church helps individuals understand and live out the ethical demands of the Law. The Church also serves as a moral compass, offering guidance on contemporary issues and advocating for justice and righteousness in society. By fostering a community committed to God's Law, the Church helps its members grow in their faith and ethical discernment.

Personal and communal obedience to God's Law is essential for a faithful Christian life. Personal obedience involves individual commitment to following God's commands in daily life. This is nurtured through spiritual disciplines such as prayer, Bible study, and fasting, which help believers grow in their relationship with God and their understanding of His will. By practicing these disciplines, individuals can develop the character and habits needed to live in accordance with God's Law.

Communal obedience, on the other hand, emphasizes the importance of community standards and accountability. Within the Church, believers support and encourage one another in their pursuit of holy living. This involves holding each other accountable to the ethical teachings of the Law and providing mutual support in times of struggle. Community standards help to maintain a collective commitment to God's Law, creating an environment where righteousness and justice can flourish.

The practical application of God's Law involves living by the Spirit, cultivating the Fruit of the Spirit, and being empowered for holy living. Ethical decision-making requires applying God's Law to contemporary issues with wisdom and discernment. The Church plays a crucial role in providing moral guidance and fostering a community committed to God's ethical standards. Personal and communal obedience are both essential, supported by spiritual disciplines and community accountability. Through these practices, believers can embody the principles of God's Law in their daily lives, reflecting His holiness, justice, and love in a tangible and transformative way.

In conclusion, the study of God's Law reveals its profound significance and enduring relevance for believers. We began by exploring the definition and importance of God's Law, understanding it as a reflection of His holy, just, and loving character. The Law serves not only as a moral compass but as a guide for living in a way that honors God and promotes human flourishing.

We traced the origin of God's Law back to the Mosaic Law and the Ten Commandments, which form the foundation of the ethical and religious life of ancient Israel. The Mosaic Covenant and the additional laws in the Torah were shown to provide a comprehensive legal and moral framework for the Israelite community. This historical context highlights the role of the Law in shaping the identity and society of God's people.

In examining the Ten Commandments, we delved into their detailed explanations and significance in Christian ethics. Each commandment reveals essential truths about human conduct and relationships, calling believers to live in a way that reflects God's righteousness. We also considered other key commandments, distinguishing between moral, ceremonial, and civil laws, and how they were fulfilled and transformed in Jesus.

The purpose of God's Law was further unpacked, demonstrating how it reveals God's character, guides moral conduct, and leads believers to Christ. The Law exposes human sinfulness and points to the necessity of grace and redemption found in Jesus. Through the Law, believers are called to a life of holiness, justice, and love, reflecting God's nature in their actions and relationships.

The New Testament perspective on the Law, particularly through the teachings of Jesus and Paul, was explored to show the continuity and transformation of the Law. Jesus' fulfillment of the Law and His emphasis on its deeper, spiritual dimensions call believers to live out its principles in a renewed and profound way. Paul's theology of justification by faith and the role of the Law in the life of a believer underscore the ongoing relevance of the Law in light of the New Covenant.

Practical application of God's Law involves living by the Spirit, which empowers believers to cultivate the Fruit of the Spirit and pursue holy living. Ethical decision-making in contemporary issues, supported by the Church's moral guidance, ensures that believers navigate the complexities of modern life with biblical wisdom. Personal and communal obedience, fostered through spiritual disciplines and community accountability, helps maintain a faithful commitment to God's ethical standards.

As we reflect on the comprehensive study of God's Law, we see that its principles are timeless and universal. God's Law continues to offer a reliable guide for moral conduct, social justice, and spiritual growth. It challenges us to live in a way that honors God and reflects His character in a world that often strays from His standards.

In light of this, I encourage you to embrace God's Law as a vital part of your faith journey. Let it guide your actions, shape your values, and inspire your relationships. Through the power of the Holy Spirit, strive to embody the principles of love, justice, and holiness in all areas of your life. By doing so, you will not only honor God but also contribute to a world that more closely mirrors His kingdom. Remember that God's Law is not a burdensome set of rules but a gracious gift that leads to true freedom and fulfillment in Christ. May you find joy and strength in living by God's Law, knowing that it reflects His perfect will and boundless love for you.

6. Embracing The Sabbath

The Sabbath holds a place of profound significance in Christian theology, serving as a symbol of rest, reflection, and divine connection. Rooted deeply in biblical tradition, the Sabbath is more than just a day of physical rest; it embodies a spiritual rhythm that aligns human life with God's creative and redemptive work. From the earliest chapters of Genesis, where God rests on the seventh day after the creation, to the detailed commandments given to the Israelites, the Sabbath emerges as a cornerstone of faith and practice.

This chapter aims to delve into the multifaceted nature of the Sabbath, tracing its origins from the creation narrative, exploring its divine purpose, and understanding its role within the context of the Ten Commandments. It will also address the historical and theological debates regarding the specific day of its observance, examining why some traditions hold to a Saturday Sabbath while others honor Sunday as a day of worship.

Furthermore, the chapter will highlight the pivotal role of the Sabbath in the formation and identity of the Seventh-day Adventist denomination, a group that has uniquely emphasized its observance. By exploring these themes, we seek to uncover the enduring relevance of the Sabbath in contemporary Christian life, offering insights into how this ancient practice continues to shape faith communities and individual believers today.

The Sabbath is fundamentally understood as a day of rest and worship, a time set apart from the regular rhythms of life to focus on spiritual renewal and connection with God. This concept of the

Sabbath is rooted deeply in the Judeo-Christian tradition and is first introduced in the biblical account of creation. In Genesis 2:1-3, after completing the work of creation in six days, God rests on the seventh day, sanctifying it as a holy day of rest. This divine rest serves as a model for humanity, establishing the pattern of a weekly Sabbath.

The significance of the Sabbath is further elaborated in the Old Testament, particularly in the laws given to the Israelites. In Exodus 20:8-11, the Fourth Commandment explicitly instructs the people to "remember the Sabbath day, to keep it holy." This commandment not only calls for cessation from labor but also emphasizes the sacredness of the day as a time dedicated to God. Similarly, in Deuteronomy 5:12-15, the Sabbath is presented as a reminder of God's deliverance of Israel from slavery in Egypt, adding a dimension of gratitude and liberation to its observance.

In the New Testament, the Sabbath continues to hold importance, though its observance is sometimes interpreted in new ways. Jesus' teachings and actions related to the Sabbath, such as healing on the Sabbath (Mark 2:27-28; Luke 13:10-17), underscore the principle that the Sabbath was made for human benefit and well-being, rather than being a burdensome legal requirement. The Apostle Paul also addresses Sabbath observance in his letters, indicating that the early Christian community grappled with the transition from Jewish Sabbath customs to new expressions of faith in Christ (Colossians 2:16-17).

Together, these biblical references outline the core understanding of the Sabbath as a divinely instituted day of rest and worship, imbued with profound spiritual significance. It is a day set apart to pause from daily toil, reflect on God's creative and redemptive work, and engage in acts of worship and compassion. The Sabbath thus serves as a perpetual reminder of God's presence, provision, and purpose for humanity.

The origins of the Sabbath are deeply rooted in the biblical narrative, beginning with the Creation account in Genesis and extending through the traditions and experiences of the Israelites. In

Genesis 2:1-3, the Sabbath is introduced as an integral part of the created order. After six days of creative activity, during which the heavens, the earth, and all living beings were formed, God rested on the seventh day. This rest was not due to fatigue but rather served as a divine cessation from creative work, signifying the completion and perfection of creation. God blessed the seventh day and made it holy, setting it apart as a time for rest and sanctification. This foundational event establishes the pattern of a weekly Sabbath, highlighting its divine origin and its role in the rhythm of life.

The significance of the Sabbath is further underscored in the context of the Israelite tradition, particularly in the narrative of Exodus 16, which recounts the provision of manna in the wilderness. As the Israelites journeyed from Egypt to the Promised Land, they faced the challenge of sustaining themselves in the desert. In response, God provided manna, a miraculous bread from heaven, to nourish them daily.

However, the provision of manna came with specific instructions that reinforced the importance of the Sabbath. The Israelites were to gather enough manna for six days, but on the sixth day, they were instructed to gather twice as much in preparation for the Sabbath, during which no manna would appear.

This practice served multiple purposes. Firstly, it tested the Israelites' obedience to God's commands and their trust in His provision. Secondly, it reinforced the rhythm of work and rest that the Sabbath was designed to establish. By refraining from gathering manna on the seventh day, the Israelites were able to dedicate the day to rest and spiritual reflection, acknowledging God's sovereignty and care. This period in the wilderness thus became a formative experience, embedding the observance of the Sabbath into the collective consciousness and religious practices of the Israelite community.

Together, these accounts from Genesis and Exodus reveal the divine intention behind the Sabbath. It is not merely a day of physical rest but a sacred time set apart for spiritual renewal and worship. The Creation account establishes its theological foundation, while the Israelite experience in the wilderness demonstrates its practical application and the blessings of obedience to God's commandments. The Sabbath thus emerges as a crucial element of the biblical narrative, shaping the faith and identity of God's people from the very beginning.

The question of why God instituted the Sabbath delves into the theological foundations that underscore its importance. At its core, the Sabbath is a divine gift designed for rest, reflection, and a deeper relationship with God. These three interconnected purposes highlight the Sabbath's role in fostering spiritual well-being and communion with the Creator.

First and foremost, the Sabbath provides a necessary rhythm of rest. Human beings, created in the image of God, are endowed with the capacity for work and creativity. However, the demands of daily life and labor can lead to physical and mental exhaustion. The Sabbath offers a reprieve, a dedicated time to cease from toil and allow the body and mind to rejuvenate. This rest is not merely physical but also spiritual, providing space to reconnect with one's inner self and with God.

Reflection is another key purpose of the Sabbath. In the busyness of life, it is easy to lose sight of the deeper questions of meaning and purpose. The Sabbath creates an intentional pause, a time to reflect on the past week, to consider one's actions, and to realign priorities according to God's will. This reflective practice is a means of spiritual growth, fostering greater awareness of God's presence and guidance.

Most importantly, the Sabbath is a time for building and nurturing a relationship with God. It is a day set apart to engage in worship, prayer, and the study of scripture. By dedicating this time to God, believers strengthen their faith and deepen their understanding of divine truths. The Sabbath thus becomes a sacred meeting point between the divine and the human, a day to experience God's love and grace more fully.

The significance of the Sabbath extends beyond individual rest and reflection. It also serves as a sign of the covenant between God and Israel, as described in Exodus 31:13-17. In this passage, God emphasizes that the Sabbath is a perpetual covenant, a sign that distinguishes the Israelites as God's chosen people. By observing the Sabbath, the Israelites affirm their identity and their commitment to the covenant relationship. It is a reminder of God's faithfulness and their own obligation to live in accordance with His commandments.

Furthermore, the concept of imitating God's rest is central to the Sabbath's theological meaning. In Genesis, God rests on the seventh day, not out of necessity, but as an example for humanity. This act of divine rest signifies the completion and perfection of creation. By observing the Sabbath, believers emulate God's rest, participating in His creative order and acknowledging His sovereignty. This imitation is an act of worship and obedience, recognizing God's authority over time and human activity. It is a declaration that life is more than work and that ultimate fulfillment is found in relationship with the Creator.

In essence, the Sabbath is a multifaceted institution with profound theological implications. It provides rest for the weary, a time for reflection and spiritual growth, and an opportunity to deepen one's relationship with God. As a sign of the covenant, it reaffirms the identity and commitment of God's people. And by imitating God's rest, believers engage in a profound act of worship and obedience, aligning their lives with the divine rhythm established at creation. Through these dimensions, the Sabbath stands as a timeless and essential element of faith, embodying God's care, covenant, and call to holiness.

The Sabbath's establishment as the Fourth Commandment within the Decalogue underscores its central role in the moral and spiritual life of the Israelites. The commandment to "Remember the Sabbath day, to keep it holy" is articulated in both Exodus 20:8-11 and Deuteronomy 5:12-15, offering a detailed rationale for its observance and highlighting its significance within the broader framework of God's law.

In Exodus 20:8-11, the Fourth Commandment is introduced with a call to remember and sanctify the Sabbath. This passage outlines the pattern of six days of labor followed by a seventh day of rest, directly linking this rhythm to the divine example set during creation. It emphasizes that the Sabbath is a day dedicated to the Lord, during which no work is to be performed by anyone within the household, including servants and animals. The rationale provided here is theological: "For in six days the Lord made the heavens and the earth, the sea, and all that is in them, but he rested on the seventh day. Therefore, the Lord blessed the Sabbath day and made it holy." This connection to creation roots the commandment in the very fabric of the cosmos, highlighting its universal and timeless nature.

In Deuteronomy 5:12-15, the Fourth Commandment is reiterated with a slight variation in emphasis. While the command to observe the Sabbath and refrain from work remains, the reasoning extends to social and redemptive dimensions. Here, the Israelites are reminded of their bondage in Egypt and God's deliverance: "Remember that you were slaves in Egypt and that the Lord your God brought you out of there with a mighty hand and an outstretched arm. Therefore the Lord your God has commanded you to observe the Sabbath day." This version of the commandment underscores the Sabbath as a symbol of liberation and divine intervention, connecting it to the collective memory of Israel's redemption.

The Sabbath's role within the Decalogue is profound, as it serves both moral and spiritual purposes. Morally, the Sabbath commandment advocates for rest and equality, ensuring that all members of society, including servants and animals, are granted respite from labor. This promotes social justice and compassion, reflecting God's care for all creation. Spiritually, the Sabbath fosters a dedicated time for worship and reflection, deepening the relationship between God and His people.

Comparing the Sabbath command with other commandments highlights its unique features. Unlike the commandments that primarily govern interpersonal relationships (such as prohibitions against murder, theft, and bearing false witness), the Fourth Commandment explicitly addresses the relationship between humanity and God. It is one of the few commandments that includes a rationale and detailed instructions, underscoring its importance. Furthermore, it bridges the two tablets of the Decalogue, which are often seen as focusing on duties to God (the first four commandments) and duties to others (the remaining six). The Sabbath commandment uniquely encompasses both dimensions: it is an act of worship and reverence toward God, and it promotes societal well-being and equity.

The Fourth Commandment's call to remember and keep the Sabbath holy stands as a distinctive and integral aspect of God's law. It not only provides a rhythm of rest and worship rooted in the creation narrative but also serves as a powerful reminder of God's deliverance and covenant with His people. By observing the Sabbath, believers affirm their commitment to God's order, justice, and compassion, making it a cornerstone of both moral conduct and spiritual devotion.

The question of which day to celebrate the Sabbath has been a topic of historical development and theological debate within Christianity. Traditionally, the Sabbath was observed on the seventh day of the week, Saturday, following the biblical creation narrative and Jewish customs. From sunset on Friday to sunset on Saturday, this day was set apart for rest and worship, as commanded in the Scriptures. This observance is deeply rooted in the Hebrew Bible, where the Sabbath is established as a day of rest in Genesis 2:2-3 and codified in the Ten Commandments in Exodus 20:8-11.

The early Christian church, emerging from a predominantly Jewish context, initially continued to observe the Sabbath on Saturday.

However, as the church grew and spread among Gentile communities, a significant shift occurred. By the second century, the Roman government and the Catholic leaders influenced many Christians to gather for worship on Sunday, the first day of the week, in honor of the resurrection of Jesus Christ, which occurred on a Sunday. This day came to be known as the Lord's Day. The shift from Saturday to Sunday worship occurred due to Satan's instruction about worshipping on a different day than the one God instituted for worship. The Roman government and the Catholic leadership were following Satan's commands against God's Law.

Despite this transition, the observance of the Sabbath on Saturday did not disappear entirely. Some Christian groups, particularly the early Jewish Christians and later the Seventh-day Adventists, maintained the seventh day as their Sabbath, emphasizing adherence to the Fourth Commandment as initially given. For these groups, observing the Sabbath on Saturday is seen as obedience to God's explicit command, rooted in the creation narrative and reaffirmed by Jesus' observance of the Sabbath.

The differing views on which day to celebrate the Sabbath have led to various debates within Christianity. Some argue that the shift to Sunday is justified by the significance of the resurrection and the early church's practice, viewing Sunday as the new Sabbath in a symbolic and theological sense. Others contend that the biblical mandate for the seventh-day Sabbath remains unchanged and that faithful obedience to God includes honoring the Sabbath on the day He initially designated Saturday.

For Seventh-day Adventists and similar denominations, the insistence on Saturday Sabbath observance is not merely about tradition but fidelity to God's commandments. They argue that the Fourth Commandment explicitly states the seventh day as a day of rest, and altering this day undermines the authority of God's law. This perspective emphasizes that obedience to God means observing the

Sabbath on the correct day as a sign of faithfulness and respect for His divine order.

In conclusion, which day to celebrate the Sabbath reflects a broader Christian dialogue about tradition, scripture, and obedience to God. While many Christian denominations have embraced Sunday as their primary day of worship, rooted in the celebration of the resurrection, others maintain that proper observance of the Sabbath as commanded by God must occur on Saturday. This debate underscores the importance of understanding the historical and theological contexts that shape religious practices and the ongoing commitment to align one's faith with the teachings and commandments of God.

The Sabbath holds a place of exceptional significance in the formation and identity of the Seventh-day Adventist denomination. This importance is rooted in the historical background of the Adventist movement, the key figures and events that led to the establishment of the Seventh-day Adventist Church, and the pivotal role the Sabbath doctrine plays in its theology and practice.

The historical background of the Seventh-day Adventist movement begins in the early 19th century with the Millerite movement, named after William Miller, a Baptist preacher who predicted the imminent return of Jesus Christ around 1843-1844. When the expected Second Coming did not occur, a period known as the Great Disappointment ensued. Out of this disillusionment, a small group of Millerites sought to understand what had gone wrong with their calculations. They turned to further Bible study, which eventually led to new insights and the foundation of the Seventh-day Adventist Church.

Key figures in the establishment of the Seventh-day Adventist Church include James White, Ellen G. White, and Joseph Bates. James White was a pivotal leader and organizer, while Ellen G. White, considered a prophetess by the church, provided much of the theological and visionary guidance that shaped the denomination. Joseph Bates, a former sea captain, played a crucial role in emphasizing the importance of the seventh-day Sabbath. Bates's advocacy for Sabbath observance was largely influenced by his interactions with Seventh Day Baptists, who had maintained the practice of Saturday worship.

The importance of the Sabbath doctrine in Seventh-day Adventist theology and practice cannot be overstated. For Adventists, the Sabbath is not merely a day of rest but a vital component of their faith and identity. It serves as a weekly reminder of God's creation, His rest on the seventh day, and His ongoing covenant with humanity. The observance of the Sabbath from Friday sunset to Saturday sunset is seen as an act of obedience to the Fourth Commandment and a sign of loyalty to God's commandments.

In Adventist theology, the Sabbath is also linked to the end-time prophecy. Ellen G. White's writings emphasize the Sabbath as a crucial test of faith in the last days, distinguishing those who follow God's commandments from those who do not. This eschatological perspective adds a layer of urgency and significance to Sabbath observance within the Adventist community.

Comparing the Seventh-day Adventist Sabbath observance with other Christian traditions reveals both unique and shared elements. While many Christian denominations, such as Roman Catholics, Orthodox Christians, and various Protestant groups, celebrate Sunday as their primary day of worship, Seventh-day Adventists adhere strictly to the biblical Sabbath on Saturday. This distinction is rooted in their interpretation of scripture and their commitment to following what they believe to be God's unaltered commandments.

Other Christian traditions may view Sunday as a fulfillment of the Sabbath, celebrating it in honor of Jesus Christ's resurrection. For them, Sunday worship is a continuation of the early Christian practice and a reflection of the new covenant established through Christ's resurrection. In contrast, Seventh-day Adventists maintain that the original Sabbath commandment has never been altered by divine authority and that true worship requires adherence to the seventh-day Sabbath as originally instituted.

In summary, the Sabbath's significance in the formation of the Seventh-day Adventist denomination is profound. The historical background of the Adventist movement, the key figures and events that led to the church's establishment, and the centrality of the Sabbath doctrine in its theology and practice highlight the unique identity and commitment of Seventh-day Adventists. By observing the Sabbath on Saturday, Adventists distinguish themselves from other Christian traditions, emphasizing their dedication to following God's commandments as they understand them. The Sabbath remains a cornerstone of their faith, symbolizing creation, covenant, and eschatological hope.

The Sabbath continues to hold relevance and significance in modern Christian life and practice, albeit with varying degrees of observance and interpretation across denominations. For many Christians, regardless of whether they observe Saturday or Sunday as their primary day of worship, the concept of setting aside a dedicated time for rest, reflection, and worship remains valuable. In a world characterized by constant activity and digital connectivity, the Sabbath offers a counter-cultural invitation to pause, disconnect from everyday routines, and reconnect with spiritual principles and community.

In contemporary society, the observance of the Sabbath presents both challenges and benefits. One of the primary challenges is the cultural shift towards a 24/7 economy and lifestyle, where work and leisure activities blend seamlessly throughout the week. This continuous busyness can make it difficult to carve out uninterrupted time for Sabbath rest and worship. Moreover, societal pressures and expectations may undervalue or even discourage taking regular periods of rest, viewing them as unproductive or unnecessary.

However, amidst these challenges, there are significant benefits to Sabbath observance. Physically, emotionally, and spiritually, the

Sabbath offers an opportunity for holistic rejuvenation. It allows individuals to recharge mentally, emotionally, and physically, reducing stress and promoting overall well-being. Spiritually, the Sabbath provides a structured time for worship, prayer, and spiritual growth, fostering deeper intimacy with God and nurturing one's faith community.

Furthermore, the Sabbath serves as a catalyst for social justice and equity. By advocating for a weekly day of rest, the Sabbath promotes the dignity and well-being of workers, emphasizing the value of work-life balance and affirming the importance of leisure, family time, and community engagement. It encourages individuals and communities to prioritize relationships, both with God and with one another, fostering a sense of interconnectedness and mutual support.

While the observance of the Sabbath faces challenges in contemporary society, its benefits are profound and multifaceted. It provides a structured rhythm of rest and worship that promotes physical, emotional, and spiritual well-being. It offers a counter-cultural witness to the importance of spiritual renewal and community connection in an increasingly busy world. By embracing the Sabbath, Christians not only honor God's commandments but also enrich their own lives and contribute to the flourishing of society as a whole.

In conclusion, this chapter has explored the multifaceted significance of the Sabbath in Christian theology and practice. We began by examining the origins of the Sabbath in the creation narrative and its establishment as the Fourth Commandment, highlighting its role as a day of rest, reflection, and relationship with God. The Sabbath's observance in the Israelite tradition, particularly in the context of the manna and wilderness experience, underscored its practical and spiritual dimensions.

We then delved into the theological reasons for God's institution of the Sabbath, emphasizing its restorative and covenantal aspects. The

Sabbath serves as a weekly opportunity to imitate God's rest, affirming His creative order and our dependence on Him. As a sign of the covenant, the Sabbath symbolizes God's ongoing relationship with His people, rooted in faithfulness and obedience.

The chapter also addressed the historical and theological debates surrounding the observance of the Sabbath, exploring the transition from Saturday to Sunday worship in some Christian traditions. We examined the Seventh-day Adventist perspective, which maintains Saturday Sabbath observance as a fundamental aspect of faith and identity, rooted in biblical commandment and prophetic interpretation.

Furthermore, we considered the contemporary relevance of the Sabbath in modern Christian life. Despite societal challenges, Sabbath observance offers tangible benefits—physical rest, spiritual renewal, and community connection—that contribute to personal well-being and social justice. In a fast-paced world, the Sabbath stands as a timeless invitation to prioritize spiritual and relational values over material pursuits.

Ultimately, the Sabbath continues to hold enduring significance for Christians today by providing a structured rhythm of worship and rest that fosters a deeper relationship with God and community. It serves as a weekly reminder of God's creative power, His redemptive work, and His call to live in harmony with His divine order. By embracing the Sabbath, Christians not only honor God's commandments but also cultivate a spirit of gratitude, compassion, and unity among believers and within society.

The Sabbath remains a sacred gift that enriches our lives, strengthens our faith, and empowers us to embody God's love in our daily interactions. As we reflect on its role in fostering spiritual growth and community engagement, may we continue to cherish and uphold the Sabbath as a cornerstone of Christian discipleship and witness in the world.

7. Managing God's Gifts

Stewardship, at its core, is the responsible management of resources that have been entrusted to one's care. From a biblical perspective, stewardship is the acknowledgment that everything we have, including our time, talents, and treasures, ultimately belongs to God. He is the Creator and owner of all, and humans are His stewards, tasked with managing His creation in a way that honors Him. This understanding is rooted in the Genesis account where humanity is given dominion over the earth to cultivate and keep it, emphasizing both responsibility and accountability.

In modern terms, stewardship extends beyond mere management to encompass a broader ethical and spiritual responsibility. It involves the wise and just use of resources, ensuring sustainability, and addressing the needs of others, reflecting God's generosity and care. This holistic view of stewardship encompasses environmental care, financial responsibility, and the nurturing of personal and communal gifts and talents. It challenges Christians to reflect God's character in all areas of life, promoting justice, compassion, and integrity.

The importance of stewardship in Christian life cannot be overstated. It is a fundamental aspect of discipleship, calling believers to live out their faith in practical ways. Stewardship is about more than giving money or volunteering time; it is about a lifestyle that prioritizes God's kingdom and purposes. It shapes our values, influences our decisions, and reflects our trust in God's provision. Proper stewardship leads to spiritual growth, strengthens community bonds, and serves as a powerful witness to the world.

FRANK M. CARAVEO

Key concepts in understanding biblical stewardship include ownership and accountability, faithfulness and diligence, and generosity and sacrifice. Recognizing God as the ultimate owner of all things reminds us of our role as caretakers who must give an account of our management. Faithfulness involves diligently using our resources and opportunities to serve God's purposes. Generosity and sacrifice are essential, reflecting the selfless love of Christ and ensuring that our stewardship benefits others and glorifies God.

In this chapter, we will explore the biblical foundation of stewardship, delve into its principles, and examine its practical implications for various aspects of life. We will also consider the challenges and misconceptions surrounding stewardship and provide practical steps to help believers live as faithful stewards. Through this exploration, we aim to deepen our understanding and commitment to managing God's gifts responsibly and joyfully.

The concept of stewardship is deeply embedded in the biblical narrative, offering a comprehensive framework for understanding our responsibility towards God's creation and His gifts. The foundation of stewardship is laid in the Old Testament and further developed in the New Testament, providing timeless principles for managing our resources.

In the Old Testament, the book of Genesis introduces the idea of stewardship with the creation mandate. Genesis 1:28-30 describes how God blessed humanity and entrusted them with dominion over the earth. This dominion is not a license for exploitation but a call to care for and cultivate creation. God commands Adam and Eve to "be fruitful and multiply and fill the earth and subdue it; and have dominion over the fish of the sea and over the birds of the heavens and over every living thing that moves on the earth." This passage underscores the responsibility of humans to manage the natural world in a way that reflects God's order and benevolence. It sets the tone for a stewardship that is marked by respect, care, and sustainability.

Leviticus 25 further elaborates on stewardship through the principles of the Sabbath Year and the Jubilee. These practices were designed to ensure the well-being of the land, the people, and the broader community. Every seventh year, the land was to rest, allowing it to recover and restore its fertility. This Sabbath Year was a reminder that the land belongs to God and that the Israelites were merely its stewards. The Year of Jubilee, observed every fiftieth year, involved the release of slaves, the return of property to its original owners, and the forgiveness of debts. These practices aimed to prevent the accumulation of wealth and power in the hands of a few, promoting economic justice and social equity. They highlighted the values of rest, restoration, and redemption, key elements of biblical stewardship.

In the New Testament, Jesus' teachings on stewardship are vividly illustrated through His parables. The Parable of the Talents in Matthew 25:14-30 is a profound example. In this parable, a master entrusts his servants with varying amounts of money before going on a journey. Upon his return, he evaluates their stewardship based on how they have managed and multiplied the resources. The servants who invested and increased their master's wealth are commended, while the servant who buried his talent out of fear is reprimanded. This parable emphasizes the importance of using God-given resources wisely and proactively. It teaches that faithful stewardship involves taking risks, making wise investments, and actively seeking to grow what has been entrusted to us.

The apostle Paul also provides valuable insights into stewardship. In 1 Corinthians 4:1-2, Paul describes himself and his fellow apostles as "servants of Christ and stewards of the mysteries of God." He underscores that the primary requirement of a steward is to be found faithful. This faithfulness is characterized by integrity, diligence, and a deep sense of responsibility towards God and His purposes. Paul's teachings reinforce that stewardship is not just about managing material resources but also about faithfully handling the spiritual truths and responsibilities entrusted to us by God.

Together, these Old and New Testament teachings form a robust biblical foundation for stewardship. They call us to recognize God's ownership of all things, to manage resources with care and wisdom, and to act with integrity and faithfulness. Understanding and embracing these principles helps us to live in a way that honors God and serves others, fulfilling our role as stewards of His creation and His gifts.

Christian stewardship is built on foundational principles that guide believers in managing God's resources with integrity, faithfulness, and generosity. These principles are grounded in the understanding of ownership and accountability, faithfulness and diligence, and generosity and sacrifice, as revealed through the Scriptures.

At the heart of Christian stewardship is the principle of ownership and accountability. Psalm 24:1 declares, "The earth is the Lord's and the fullness thereof, the world and those who dwell therein." This verse clearly establishes that God is the ultimate owner of everything. Everything we have, including our lives, resources, and abilities, belongs to Him. This understanding shifts our perspective from seeing ourselves as owners to recognizing our role as stewards or caretakers. We are entrusted with God's creation and resources, and we are called to manage them responsibly and wisely.

Human responsibility and accountability are closely linked to this principle. Romans 14:12 reminds us, "So then each of us will give an account of himself to God." This accountability underscores that we will one day stand before God and account for how we have managed His resources. This accountability is not limited to financial resources but extends to our time, talents, and even our relationships. It calls us to live with a sense of responsibility, knowing that our actions have eternal significance.

Faithfulness and diligence are essential aspects of stewardship. The Parable of the Faithful Steward in Luke 12:42-48 illustrates this principle vividly. In this parable, Jesus describes a servant whom the master puts in charge of his household to give them their food at the proper time. The faithful and wise steward is blessed when the master finds him doing his duty upon his return. Conversely, the servant who abuses his position and mistreats others is severely punished. This parable emphasizes that faithful stewardship involves being diligent and trustworthy in fulfilling our responsibilities, even when we think no one is watching. It is about consistently doing what is right and good, regardless of external recognition or reward.

Generosity and sacrifice are also core principles of Christian stewardship. The story of the Widow's Offering in Mark 12:41-44 poignantly illustrates these values. Jesus observes a poor widow putting two small copper coins into the temple treasury. Despite the small monetary value of her offering, Jesus commends her because she gave out of her poverty, sacrificing everything she had to live on. This act of sacrificial giving highlights that true generosity is measured not by the amount given but by the heart and sacrifice behind it. It challenges us to give selflessly and sacrificially, trusting that God will provide for our needs.

The principles of tithing and offerings further underscore the importance of generosity in stewardship. Malachi 3:10 exhorts, "Bring the full tithe into the storehouse, that there may be food in my house. And thereby put me to the test, says the Lord of hosts, if I will not open the windows of heaven for you and pour down for you a blessing until there is no more need." Tithing, the practice of giving a tenth of one's income, and offerings, which are additional gifts, are ways believers honor God with their resources. These practices acknowledge God's provision and cultivate a spirit of gratitude and trust. They also support the work of the church and its mission, ensuring that God's work continues and flourishes.

Together, these principles form a comprehensive approach to Christian stewardship. They call us to recognize God's ownership of all things, to manage resources with faithfulness and diligence, and to practice generosity and sacrifice. Embracing these principles enables us to live as faithful stewards, honoring God with our lives and resources, and contributing to His kingdom's growth and impact in the world.

Stewardship encompasses the responsible management of various resources God has entrusted to us. These resources include time, talents and skills, finances, and the environment. Each of these areas offers unique opportunities to honor God and serve others, reflecting our commitment to faithful stewardship.

Time is one of the most valuable resources we possess, and prioritizing time with God is essential. Psalm 90:12 teaches us to "number our days that we may get a heart of wisdom." This verse emphasizes the importance of recognizing the brevity of life and using our time wisely. Prioritizing time with God involves setting aside moments for prayer, meditation, and studying Scripture.

It is through these practices that we deepen our relationship with God and gain the wisdom needed to navigate life's challenges. Additionally, Exodus 20:8-11 instructs us to balance work, rest, and worship. The Sabbath commandment reminds us to set apart one day each week for rest and worship, reflecting on God's goodness and provision. This balance ensures that we are not consumed by our work and that we dedicate time to spiritual renewal and physical rest.

Our talents and skills are another vital area of stewardship. According to 1 Peter 4:10-11, "As each has received a gift, use it to serve one another, as good stewards of God's varied grace: whoever speaks, as one who speaks oracles of God; whoever serves, as one who serves by the strength that God supplies." This passage encourages us to use our God-given abilities to glorify Him and serve others. Each person's unique gifts contribute to the body of Christ, and it is our responsibility to develop and utilize these talents within our communities. Encouraging and developing talents in the church community fosters a culture of growth and mutual support. By identifying and nurturing the abilities of others, we build a stronger, more vibrant community that can effectively carry out God's mission.

Financial stewardship is also a critical aspect of managing our resources. Proverbs 3:9-10 advises, "Honor the Lord with your wealth and with the first fruits of all your produce; then your barns will be filled with plenty, and your vats will be bursting with wine."

This wisdom literature highlights the principle of honoring God with our finances, recognizing that everything we have comes from Him. Practicing sound money management includes budgeting, saving, and avoiding unnecessary debt, as taught in Romans 13:8: "Owe no one anything, except to love each other, for the one who loves another has fulfilled the law." This principle encourages us to live within our means and avoid the burdens of debt, which can hinder our ability to be generous. Practicing generosity involves giving to those in need and supporting the work of the church, reflecting God's love and provision through our financial resources.

Environmental stewardship is another crucial area where we can demonstrate our commitment to God's creation. Genesis 2:15 describes how God placed Adam in the Garden of Eden "to work it and keep it," highlighting humanity's responsibility to care for the environment. This call to stewardship means we must manage natural resources wisely, ensuring sustainability for future generations. Christian responsibility in environmental stewardship involves advocating for policies and practices that protect the environment, reducing waste, and promoting conservation efforts. By caring for God's creation, we honor the Creator and contribute to the well-being of the planet and its inhabitants.

In summary, stewardship of resources involves the mindful and responsible management of time, talents and skills, finances, and the environment. Prioritizing time with God, balancing work and rest, using our gifts for His glory, managing finances according to biblical principles, and caring for the environment are all integral aspects of living as faithful stewards. Embracing these practices helps us fulfill our God-given responsibilities, bringing glory to Him and fostering a flourishing, just, and sustainable world.

Stewardship profoundly impacts the life of a Christian, influencing spiritual growth and maturity, fostering community and relationships, and enhancing witness and evangelism. By managing God's gifts responsibly, believers can experience personal transformation, strengthen their faith communities, and effectively share God's love with the world.

Spiritual growth and maturity are significant outcomes of faithful stewardship. In Matthew 6:19-21, Jesus teaches, "Do not lay up for yourselves treasures on earth, where moth and rust destroy and where thieves break in and steal, but lay up for yourselves treasures in heaven... For where your treasure is, there your heart will be also."

This passage challenges us to develop trust in God rather than in material wealth. By focusing on heavenly treasures, we cultivate a deeper reliance on God's provision and faithfulness. Stewardship encourages us to invest in spiritual growth, leading to a more profound understanding of God's character and His purposes for our lives. Hebrews 11:6 further emphasizes that "without faith it is impossible to please Him, for whoever would draw near to God must believe that He exists and that He rewards those who seek Him." Faithful stewardship nurtures our faith, prompting us to obey God's commands and trust in His promises. As we grow in faith and obedience, we experience greater spiritual maturity and alignment with God's will.

Community and relationships are also strengthened through stewardship. Acts 2:44-45 describe the early church's practice of sharing resources: "And all who believed were together and had all things in common. And they were selling their possessions and belongings and distributing the proceeds to all, as any had need." This communal approach to resources fosters unity and support within the church, ensuring that everyone's needs are met. Stewardship promotes a culture of generosity and care, where members actively contribute to the well-being of the community.

Additionally, Galatians 5:13 exhorts believers to "serve one another humbly in love." Acts of service, whether through volunteering time, sharing skills, or providing financial support, build strong, loving relationships within the church. These acts of service create a supportive network, reinforcing the sense of belonging and mutual care among believers.

Stewardship also significantly impacts witness and evangelism. By demonstrating God's love through stewardship, Christians can be a light to the world. In Matthew 5:16, Jesus encourages His followers, "Let your light shine before others, so that they may see your good works and give glory to your Father who is in heaven." Faithful stewardship, marked by generosity, integrity, and compassion, reflects God's character and draws others to Him. When Christians manage their resources wisely and use them to bless others, they provide a powerful testimony of God's love and provision. Furthermore, stewardship supports missions and outreach, extending the impact of the gospel.

Philippians 4:15-18 highlights the importance of financial support for missionary work. Paul commends the Philippians for their partnership in giving and receiving, which enabled his ministry to flourish. By using resources to support missions and outreach, Christians can help spread the gospel to unreached areas, providing tangible expressions of God's love and transforming lives.

In conclusion, the impact of stewardship on Christian life is multifaceted, promoting spiritual growth and maturity, strengthening community and relationships, and enhancing witness and evangelism. By developing trust in God, growing in faith and obedience, fostering unity through shared resources, building relationships through acts of service, and demonstrating God's love through stewardship, believers can live out their faith in meaningful and transformative ways. Embracing stewardship not only honors God but also enriches our lives and communities, advancing His kingdom on earth.

Stewardship, while foundational to Christian life, is not without its challenges and misconceptions. Understanding these obstacles can help believers navigate them effectively, ensuring their stewardship aligns with biblical principles.

One of the primary misconceptions in stewardship is misunderstanding ownership. Many people fall into the trap of materialism, believing that accumulating wealth and possessions will bring satisfaction and security. 1 Timothy 6:10 warns, "For the love of money is a root of all kinds of evils. It is through this craving that some have wandered away from the faith and pierced themselves with many pangs."

This verse highlights how materialism can divert our focus from God, leading to spiritual decline and personal distress. Another prevalent misconception is the myth of self-sufficiency. James 4:13-15 addresses this, stating, "Come now, you who say, 'Today or tomorrow we will go into such and such a town and spend a year there and trade and make a profit'—yet you do not know what tomorrow will bring. What is your life? For you are a mist that appears for a little time and then vanishes. Instead, you ought to say, 'If the Lord wills, we will live and do this or that.'" This passage reminds us that our plans and successes depend on God's will, not our own abilities. Believing in self-sufficiency can lead to arrogance and a lack of reliance on God.

Misuse of resources is another significant challenge in stewardship. Poor financial decisions can have detrimental spiritual impacts. Proverbs 21:20 observes, "Precious treasure and oil are in a wise man's dwelling, but a foolish man devours it." This proverb illustrates how mismanagement of resources can lead to loss and hardship.

When we fail to manage our finances wisely, we not only jeopardize our material well-being but also hinder our ability to support God's work and assist others. Neglecting God-given talents and opportunities is another form of resource misuse. In the Parable of the Talents (Matthew 25:24-30), Jesus recounts how a servant, out of fear and laziness, buried the talent entrusted to him instead of investing it. The master condemns this servant for wasting the opportunity to generate more value. This parable underscores the importance of actively using our gifts and opportunities to serve God and others. Neglecting them can result in missed blessings and potential growth.

Overcoming these challenges requires trusting in God's provision and seeking wisdom and counsel. Philippians 4:19 assures us, "And my God will supply every need of yours according to his riches in glory in Christ Jesus." Trusting in God's provision helps us resist the temptation of materialism and the fear of insufficiency. It reminds us that our true security lies in God's faithfulness, not in our possessions or abilities. Seeking wisdom and counsel is also vital. Proverbs 11:14 states, "Where there is no guidance, a people falls, but in an abundance of counselors there is safety." Seeking advice from trusted spiritual leaders and wise individuals can help us make better decisions and avoid pitfalls. This counsel can provide insights and accountability, helping us to steward our resources effectively and align our actions with God's will.

In summary, challenges and misconceptions in stewardship can hinder our ability to manage God's resources wisely. Misunderstanding ownership, falling into the traps of materialism and self-sufficiency, and misusing resources through poor financial decisions or neglecting talents all pose significant obstacles. However, by trusting in God's provision and seeking wisdom and counsel, we can overcome these challenges and fulfill our role as faithful stewards. Embracing these truths enables us to live in a way that honors God, benefits others, and fosters spiritual growth and maturity.

Implementing faithful stewardship in daily life involves intentional planning, family involvement, and active engagement with the church. These practical steps help ensure that our management of resources reflects our commitment to God and His principles.

Developing a stewardship plan is a foundational step. Setting spiritual and financial goals helps to align our actions with our values and priorities. Spiritual goals might include dedicating specific times for prayer and Bible study, participating in ministry activities, or committing to regular church attendance. Financial goals could involve tithing consistently, saving for future needs, or reducing debt. Creating a budget is crucial for achieving these financial goals. A budget helps track income and expenses, ensuring that spending aligns with priorities and preventing unnecessary debt. Tracking expenses regularly can highlight spending patterns and areas where adjustments are needed, fostering better financial management and enabling more generous giving.

Involving the family in stewardship practices is essential for cultivating a culture of responsible resource management. Teaching children about stewardship from an early age is a key component. Deuteronomy 6:6-7 instructs, "And these words that I command you today shall be on your heart. You shall teach them diligently to your children, and shall talk of them when you sit in your house, and when you walk by the way, and when you lie down, and when you rise." This passage emphasizes the importance of imparting biblical principles to the next generation. Parents can teach children about the value of money, the importance of giving, and the joy of helping others. Modeling stewardship in family decisions reinforces these lessons. For example, involving children in discussions about charitable giving, explaining budget choices, and demonstrating responsible spending habits can provide practical examples of stewardship in action. This modeling helps children understand that stewardship is an integral part of life, rooted in faith and responsibility.

Engaging with the church is another vital aspect of faithful stewardship. Participating in stewardship programs and initiatives offered by the church can provide valuable resources and support. These programs often include workshops, seminars, and classes on financial management, generosity, and the biblical principles of stewardship. By participating, individuals and families can gain practical skills and insights to enhance their stewardship practices. Supporting church projects and missions is another way to engage with the church community. Financially contributing to church initiatives, volunteering time and talents, and participating in mission trips or outreach programs are all expressions of stewardship. These activities not only support the church's work but also foster a sense of community and shared purpose.

In conclusion, practical steps to faithful stewardship involve developing a stewardship plan, involving the family, and engaging with the church. Setting spiritual and financial goals, creating a budget, and tracking expenses provide a framework for responsible resource management. Teaching children about stewardship and modeling these principles in family decisions cultivate a culture of stewardship within the home. Participating in church stewardship programs and supporting church projects and missions enhance communal engagement and collective impact. By taking these practical steps, believers can honor God with their resources, grow in their faith, and contribute to the flourishing of their communities and the advancement of God's kingdom.

In this exploration of stewardship, we have journeyed through its biblical foundation, principles, practical applications, and the impact it has on Christian life. We have seen that stewardship is fundamentally about recognizing God's ownership of everything, managing His resources wisely, and using them to glorify Him and serve others. Key points include the importance of understanding ownership and accountability, practicing faithfulness and diligence, and embodying generosity and sacrifice. We have also discussed the management of various resources—time, talents, finances, and the environment—highlighting how responsible stewardship in these areas reflects our commitment to God's kingdom.

Stewardship is not just a duty but a privilege. It is an opportunity to grow spiritually, deepen our trust in God, and experience the joy of giving and serving. By prioritizing time with God, using our gifts for His glory, managing finances according to biblical principles, and caring for the environment, we honor God and contribute to His work on earth. Engaging in stewardship builds strong, supportive communities and allows us to witness God's love through our actions.

As we conclude, let us be encouraged to embrace stewardship wholeheartedly. It is a transformative practice that shapes our character, strengthens our relationships, and enhances our witness to the world. Stewardship invites us to live with intentionality, gratitude, and generosity, recognizing that everything we have is a gift from God.

Therefore, let us respond to this call to action: living as faithful stewards. Let us commit to setting spiritual and financial goals, creating budgets, and tracking our expenses. Let us teach our children the value of stewardship and model it in our family decisions. Let us engage with our church communities, participating in stewardship programs and supporting projects and missions. By doing so, we align our lives with God's purposes and contribute to the flourishing of His kingdom.

May we each strive to be faithful stewards, using the resources God has entrusted to us for His glory and the good of others. In doing so, we will not only fulfill our responsibilities but also experience the abundant life that comes from living according to God's design.

8. Living a Christ-Centered Life

Christian behavior, often referred to as Christian conduct or ethics, encompasses the attitudes, actions, and lifestyle choices that align with the teachings of Jesus Christ. At its core, Christian behavior is about embodying the principles and values of the Christian faith in every aspect of life. This involves a commitment to living in a way that reflects the character of Christ, striving for holiness, and serving as a witness to others through our actions.

The importance of Christian behavior cannot be overstated. It is the tangible expression of faith, the visible manifestation of an inward transformation brought about by a relationship with Jesus. Our conduct as Christians serves as a testimony to the world, illustrating the transformative power of the gospel. When believers live according to biblical principles, they demonstrate the love, grace, and truth of God, drawing others to Him. Additionally, Christian behavior fosters personal growth and spiritual maturity, helping individuals to develop Christ-like character and deepening their relationship with God.

The foundation for Christian conduct is firmly rooted in Scripture. The Bible provides clear guidance on how believers are to live, offering both specific commandments and overarching principles that govern our behavior. Jesus' teachings, particularly the Sermon on the Mount, set forth a radical vision of righteousness that calls His followers to exceed mere legalistic observance and to embody the spirit of God's law in their hearts and actions.

In the Old Testament, the Ten Commandments serve as a foundational ethical code, outlining fundamental moral imperatives such as honesty, purity, and respect for others. These commandments highlight the necessity of love for God and love for neighbor, which Jesus affirmed as the greatest commandments, encapsulating the essence of the law and the prophets.

The New Testament builds upon these foundations, emphasizing the role of the Holy Spirit in guiding and empowering believers to live in accordance with God's will. The apostle Paul, in his letters, provides extensive instruction on Christian conduct, urging believers to put off their old selves and to be renewed in the spirit of their minds, putting on the new self created after the likeness of God in true righteousness and holiness. Paul's writings also highlight the fruit of the Spirit—qualities such as love, joy, peace, patience, kindness, goodness, faithfulness, gentleness, and self-control—as markers of a life transformed by the Spirit.

In summary, Christian behavior is an integral aspect of the Christian faith, reflecting the teachings of Scripture and the transformative power of a relationship with Jesus Christ. It serves as a witness to the world, a pathway to spiritual growth, and a means of embodying the love and truth of God in everyday life. Through the guidance of the Holy Spirit and the foundational principles found in the Bible, believers are called to live lives that honor God and reflect His character to those around them.

The call to holiness is a central theme in the Christian life, inviting believers to reflect the purity and righteousness of God in every aspect of their being. Understanding holiness begins with recognizing its significance in the Bible. Holiness, in its essence, means to be set apart for God, to live in a manner that is distinct from the ways of the world, and to embody the moral and ethical standards established by God. Throughout Scripture, holiness is depicted as both a divine attribute and a human calling. God is described as holy, emphasizing His absolute purity, moral perfection, and separateness from sin. As God's people, believers are called to mirror His holiness, striving to live lives that honor and glorify Him.

In the Old Testament, the concept of holiness is prominently featured. The nation of Israel was chosen by God to be a holy people, set apart to reflect His character and to serve as a light to the nations. The book of Leviticus, in particular, outlines various laws and regulations designed to maintain the holiness of the Israelites, emphasizing the importance of purity in worship, conduct, and community life. The repeated refrain, "Be holy, for I am holy," encapsulates the call for God's people to align themselves with His nature.

In the New Testament, the call to holiness is reiterated and expanded. Jesus' life and teachings provide the ultimate model of holiness, demonstrating how to live in perfect obedience to God's will. His example challenges believers to pursue a higher standard of righteousness that transcends mere external compliance and penetrates the heart and mind. The apostle Peter echoes this call, urging believers to be holy in all their conduct, just as God who called them is holy.

The practical aspects of holiness in daily life involve a deliberate and continuous effort to align one's thoughts, words, and actions with God's standards. This includes practicing virtues such as honesty, integrity, kindness, and compassion, and avoiding behaviors that are contrary to God's will, such as deceit, immorality, and selfishness. Holiness also entails a commitment to spiritual disciplines like prayer, Bible study, and worship, which foster a deeper relationship with God and provide strength to resist temptation.

Living a holy life requires vigilance and intentionality. It involves making choices that reflect one's commitment to God, even when those choices are difficult or counter-cultural. It means seeking to honor God in every sphere of life—whether at home, work, or in social interactions—and striving to be a positive influence on others through one's conduct.

FRANK M. CARAVEO

The role of the Holy Spirit in sanctification is crucial. Sanctification is the process by which believers are gradually transformed into the likeness of Christ, growing in holiness and spiritual maturity. The Holy Spirit, who indwells every believer, is the agent of this transformation. He convicts of sin, guides into truth, and empowers for righteous living. The Spirit's work in sanctification is both instantaneous and progressive: believers are positionally sanctified at the moment of salvation, declared holy by virtue of their union with Christ, and they are progressively sanctified over the course of their lives as they cooperate with the Spirit's leading.

The Holy Spirit's role in sanctification involves several key functions. He illuminates the Scriptures, enabling believers to understand and apply God's Word to their lives. He produces the fruit of the Spirit, cultivating Christ-like qualities in believers' character. He also provides the strength and resolve needed to overcome sinful tendencies and to pursue godly living. Through the Spirit's power, believers are able to resist temptation, grow in virtue, and reflect the holiness of God in ever-increasing measure.

In summary, the call to holiness is a foundational aspect of the Christian life, rooted in the character of God and exemplified in the life of Jesus. Understanding holiness involves recognizing its biblical significance and its practical implications for daily living. The pursuit of holiness requires a committed effort to align one's life with God's standards and to cultivate a relationship with Him through spiritual disciplines. The Holy Spirit plays an indispensable role in this process, empowering believers to grow in holiness and to reflect the character of Christ in all they do.

The Fruit of the Spirit, as outlined in Galatians 5:22-23, represents the qualities and virtues that the Holy Spirit cultivates in the lives of believers. These attributes are essential markers of a life transformed by Christ and empowered by the Spirit. They serve as a tangible demonstration of God's presence within us and provide a framework for Christian behavior that reflects the character of Jesus. The Fruit of the Spirit encompasses love, joy, peace, patience, kindness, goodness, faithfulness, gentleness, and self-control, each playing a crucial role in the believer's journey toward spiritual maturity.

Love is the foremost fruit and the foundation of all the others. It is an unconditional, selfless affection that seeks the best for others, mirroring the love of Christ. This love is not limited to those who are easy to love but extends to everyone, including enemies and those who may be difficult to love. It is expressed through acts of kindness, compassion, and a willingness to forgive. In practical terms, love involves putting others' needs above our own, serving selflessly, and demonstrating care and concern in everyday interactions.

Joy is a deep-seated sense of happiness and contentment that is rooted in a relationship with God, independent of external circumstances. This joy transcends temporary pleasures and remains steadfast even in trials. It is the result of understanding and embracing God's love, grace, and promises. Practically, joy is cultivated by maintaining a thankful heart, focusing on God's blessings, and finding delight in His presence through worship, prayer, and fellowship.

Peace is an inner tranquility and assurance that comes from trusting in God's sovereignty and faithfulness. It is the calm that prevails in the midst of life's storms, grounded in the confidence that God is in control. This peace guards our hearts and minds, enabling us to remain steady and composed. Practically, peace is fostered by casting our anxieties on God, meditating on His Word, and seeking to reconcile and maintain harmonious relationships with others.

Patience, or long-suffering, is the ability to endure difficult situations and to tolerate the shortcomings of others without becoming frustrated or angry. It reflects God's patience with us and calls us to extend the same grace to others. Practically, patience is exercised by maintaining a calm and forgiving attitude, avoiding rash reactions, and persevering through challenges with a steadfast spirit.

Kindness is a gentle, considerate, and compassionate approach to others, reflecting the kindness of God. It involves acting in ways that benefit and uplift those around us. Practically, kindness is demonstrated through simple acts of generosity, speaking words of encouragement, and being attentive to the needs of others.

Goodness is moral integrity and uprightness, characterized by a desire to do what is right and to reflect God's righteousness in our actions. It is an active pursuit of virtue and moral excellence. Practically, goodness is lived out by making ethical choices, standing up for justice, and being honest and fair in our dealings with others.

Faithfulness is steadfast loyalty and reliability in our relationship with God and others. It involves being trustworthy, dependable, and consistent in our commitments. Practically, faithfulness is shown by keeping our promises, being diligent in our responsibilities, and remaining true to our faith even in the face of adversity.

Gentleness, or meekness, is strength under control. It is a humble and gentle demeanor that is neither harsh nor aggressive. It involves treating others with respect and consideration. Practically, gentleness is expressed by responding to others with a soft and understanding approach, avoiding harsh criticism, and being patient and empathetic in our interactions.

Self-control is the ability to regulate one's desires, impulses, and behaviors. It is the discipline to make choices that align with God's will rather than succumbing to selfish or sinful inclinations. Practically, self-control is maintained by setting boundaries, practicing restraint, and seeking God's help to overcome temptations.

The practical application of the Fruit of the Spirit involves intentionally integrating these qualities into our daily lives. This requires a conscious effort to align our actions and attitudes with the character of Christ, seeking the Holy Spirit's guidance and empowerment. It means being mindful of how we interact with others, striving to be a positive influence, and reflecting God's love and grace in all we do. By allowing the Fruit of the Spirit to flourish within us, we not only grow in spiritual maturity but also become effective witnesses to the transformative power of the gospel. Through our words and deeds, we demonstrate the beauty of a life surrendered to God and inspire others to seek the same.

Ethical living, as guided by Scripture, encompasses a commitment to aligning one's actions and decisions with the moral principles and values set forth in the Bible. This adherence to biblical ethics serves as a testament to the transformative power of faith and as a reflection of God's character. Key aspects of ethical living according to Scripture include honesty and integrity, sexual purity, compassion and generosity, and responsibility and work ethic.

Honesty and integrity are foundational to ethical living. The Bible consistently emphasizes the importance of truthfulness and moral uprightness. Proverbs 12:22 states, "The Lord detests lying lips, but he delights in people who are trustworthy." Honesty involves being truthful in our words and actions, avoiding deceit, and being transparent in our dealings with others. Integrity goes further, encompassing a wholeness of character where one's actions consistently reflect their values and beliefs. Living with integrity means being the same person in private as we are in public, maintaining moral consistency, and upholding our commitments. Practically, this means confessing when we are wrong, being forthright in our communications, and striving to earn the trust of others through our reliability and sincerity.

Sexual purity is another critical component of ethical living according to Scripture. The Bible calls believers to honor God with their bodies, maintaining purity in thoughts, words, and actions. 1 Thessalonians 4:3-5 instructs, "It is God's will that you should be sanctified: that you should avoid sexual immorality; that each of you should learn to control your own body in a way that is holy and honorable, not in passionate lust like the pagans, who do not know

God." Sexual purity involves abstaining from behaviors that deviate from God's design for sexuality, which is intended to be expressed within the covenant of marriage between a man and a woman. Practically, this includes guarding against inappropriate relationships, avoiding sexually explicit content, and cultivating a mindset that respects the sanctity of the marital relationship. By pursuing sexual purity, believers honor God's intention for human relationships and uphold the dignity of themselves and others.

Compassion and generosity are essential expressions of ethical living, reflecting God's heart for the vulnerable and the needy. The Bible repeatedly calls believers to show kindness and to care for those in need. Colossians 3:12 encourages, "Therefore, as God's chosen people, holy and dearly loved, clothe yourselves with compassion, kindness, humility, gentleness and patience." Compassion involves empathizing with others, feeling their pain, and being moved to action on their behalf. Generosity goes hand in hand with compassion, prompting us to share our resources, time, and talents with those in need. Practically, this means supporting charitable causes, volunteering, and offering help to those who are struggling. By embodying compassion and generosity, believers reflect the love and mercy of God, creating a ripple effect of kindness and support within their communities.

Responsibility and work ethic are also crucial aspects of ethical living. The Bible teaches that work is a divine calling and that believers should approach their tasks with diligence and excellence. Colossians 3:23-24 advises, "Whatever you do, work at it with all your heart, as working for the Lord, not for human masters, since you know that you will receive an inheritance from the Lord as a reward.

It is the Lord Christ you are serving." Responsibility involves being accountable for our actions, fulfilling our obligations, and managing our resources wisely. A strong work ethic means performing our duties with dedication, striving for excellence, and viewing our work as an opportunity to honor God. Practically, this means being punctual,

TRUE PRINCIPLES OF CHRISTIANITY BOOK TWO

reliable, and industrious in our professional and personal endeavors. By demonstrating responsibility and a robust work ethic, believers contribute positively to their workplaces and communities, setting an example of integrity and commitment.

In summary, ethical living according to Scripture involves a comprehensive approach to morality that encompasses honesty and integrity, sexual purity, compassion and generosity, and responsibility and work ethic. By adhering to these biblical principles, believers reflect the character of God, foster trust and respect in their relationships, and create a positive impact on their communities. Ethical living is a testament to the transformative power of faith, providing a tangible demonstration of the gospel's influence in every aspect of life. Through their ethical conduct, believers bear witness to the love, grace, and truth of God, inviting others to experience the same transformative relationship with Him.

Interpersonal relationships are a vital aspect of the Christian life, reflecting the communal nature of the faith and the relational character of God. The Bible provides extensive guidance on how believers are to interact with others, emphasizing love, forgiveness, humility, service, conflict resolution, and reconciliation. These principles form the foundation of healthy and God-honoring relationships.

Love and forgiveness are at the heart of Christian relationships. Jesus commanded His followers to love one another as He has loved them, setting a high standard of selfless, sacrificial love. This love extends beyond friends and family to include neighbors, strangers, and even enemies. It is an active love that seeks the well-being of others and is demonstrated through acts of kindness, compassion, and generosity. Forgiveness is closely tied to love and is essential for maintaining healthy relationships. Jesus taught that just as God has forgiven us, we must also forgive those who have wronged us. Forgiveness involves letting go of resentment and the desire for revenge, choosing instead to extend grace and seek reconciliation. It is a powerful expression of love that heals wounds, restores relationships, and reflects the forgiving nature of God.

Humility and service are also crucial components of Christian relationships. The Bible calls believers to emulate the humility of Christ, who, despite His divine nature, took on the form of a servant and gave His life for others. Humility involves recognizing our own limitations and valuing others above ourselves. It means being willing to listen, learn, and admit when we are wrong.

Service flows naturally from humility, prompting us to meet the needs of others without seeking recognition or reward. Jesus demonstrated this through His life and teachings, urging His followers to serve one another in love. In practical terms, humility and service are expressed through acts of kindness, volunteering, and supporting those in need. By adopting a servant's heart, believers foster an environment of mutual respect and care, strengthening the bonds of community and reflecting the love of Christ.

Conflict resolution and reconciliation are essential for maintaining peace and unity within relationships. Conflicts are inevitable, but the Bible provides principles for addressing and resolving them in a healthy and constructive manner. Jesus taught that reconciliation should be a priority, urging believers to seek resolution quickly and to take the initiative in making peace.

This involves approaching conflicts with a spirit of humility, seeking to understand the perspectives of others, and being willing to forgive and ask for forgiveness. Effective conflict resolution requires open and honest communication, active listening, and a commitment to finding mutually acceptable solutions. Reconciliation goes beyond resolving disputes; it seeks to restore and strengthen relationships, fostering a deeper sense of unity and trust. By practicing these principles, believers can navigate conflicts in a way that honors God and promotes harmony within their communities.

In summary, interpersonal relationships in the Christian context are built on the principles of love and forgiveness, humility and service, and conflict resolution and reconciliation. These biblical teachings guide believers in fostering healthy, respectful, and supportive relationships that reflect the character of God. Through love and forgiveness, believers demonstrate the selfless, unconditional love of Christ, creating an environment of grace and healing. Humility and service cultivate a spirit of mutual care and respect, encouraging believers to support and uplift one another. Conflict resolution and reconciliation promote peace and unity, enabling believers to navigate disagreements in a way that strengthens relationships and honors God. By adhering to these principles, believers bear witness to the transformative power of the gospel in their relationships, inviting others to experience the same love and grace that they have received from God.

Social and cultural engagement is an important aspect of living out the Christian faith in a world that is diverse and multifaceted. Believers are called to actively participate in society, bringing the light of the gospel into every sphere of life while maintaining their spiritual values. This involves embracing the responsibility to contribute positively to society, balancing cultural participation with a steadfast commitment to biblical principles, and witnessing through behavior that reflects the character of Christ.

Christian responsibility in society stems from the biblical mandate to love our neighbors and seek the common good. Believers are called to be salt and light in the world, influencing their communities and cultures in ways that promote justice, compassion, and righteousness. This responsibility includes advocating for the marginalized, caring for the poor, and working towards solutions to social issues such as inequality, injustice, and environmental stewardship. Christians are to engage in their communities through various means, such as volunteering, participating in civic activities, and supporting initiatives that align with biblical values. By doing so, they fulfill their calling to be agents of God's kingdom, demonstrating His love and justice in tangible ways.

Balancing cultural participation with spiritual values is a nuanced endeavor that requires discernment and intentionality. While Christians are called to engage with the world, they must do so without compromising their faith. This balance involves critically evaluating cultural trends and practices through the lens of Scripture, embracing those that are compatible with Christian values and rejecting those that are contrary to God's will.

It also means being mindful of the influences we allow into our lives, ensuring that they do not lead us away from our commitment to Christ. Engaging with culture in a balanced way includes participating in the arts, media, and entertainment in ways that are edifying and that promote positive messages. It also involves engaging in respectful dialogue with those who hold different beliefs, seeking common ground while standing firm in one's faith. By navigating cultural participation with wisdom and grace, Christians can effectively witness to the transformative power of the gospel.

Witnessing through behavior is a powerful form of social and cultural engagement. Actions often speak louder than words, and the way Christians conduct themselves can profoundly impact those around them. Living out the values of the gospel in everyday life serves as a testament to the reality of God's presence and power.

This means exhibiting the Fruit of the Spirit—love, joy, peace, patience, kindness, goodness, faithfulness, gentleness, and self-control—in all interactions. It involves practicing honesty and integrity, showing compassion and generosity, and being reliable and diligent in our responsibilities. By embodying these virtues, Christians can inspire others and draw them toward the faith. Furthermore, witnessing through behavior includes addressing societal issues with a Christ-like attitude, advocating for justice, and showing empathy and support to those in need. This approach not only demonstrates the practical implications of the gospel but also opens doors for meaningful conversations about faith.

In summary, social and cultural engagement for Christians involves a commitment to influencing society positively while upholding spiritual values. It requires embracing the responsibility to contribute to the common good, balancing cultural participation with biblical principles, and witnessing through behavior that reflects Christ's love and righteousness. By engaging in society in these ways, believers can make a meaningful impact, showcasing the transformative power of the gospel and inviting others to experience the hope and love found in a relationship with Jesus. Through their actions and attitudes, Christians have the opportunity to be a beacon of light in a world in need of God's truth and grace.

In the digital age, Christian behavior extends into the realm of online interactions, where social media and other digital platforms have become integral parts of daily life. Navigating these spaces with wisdom and integrity is essential for maintaining a witness that honors God. This involves thoughtful engagement on social media, upholding Christian values in online interactions, and leveraging digital platforms for evangelism while addressing the inherent challenges.

Navigating social media and online interactions requires discernment and intentionality. Social media can be a powerful tool for connection, but it also presents numerous pitfalls. Christians are called to engage these platforms in a manner that reflects their faith, avoiding behaviors that undermine their witness. This means being mindful of the content we consume and share, ensuring it aligns with biblical values. It involves promoting positivity, encouragement, and truth rather than spreading negativity, misinformation, or divisive content. Online interactions should be characterized by respect, kindness, and empathy, even in the face of disagreement. By doing so, believers can foster a digital presence that reflects the love and grace of Christ.

Maintaining integrity and witness online is crucial in an environment where anonymity can sometimes lead to a lapse in moral standards. Christians must remember that their online presence is an extension of their witness. This means being honest and transparent in all communications, avoiding deceitful practices such as spreading false information or misrepresenting oneself. It also involves being consistent in behavior both online and offline, ensuring that one's digital persona does not contradict their real-life values.

Upholding integrity online includes resisting the temptation to engage in gossip, slander, or inappropriate content. Instead, believers should use their online platforms to promote justice, share uplifting messages, and offer support and encouragement to others. By maintaining integrity, Christians can build trust and respect, making their witness more effective and credible.

The challenges and opportunities of digital evangelism present unique considerations for Christians seeking to spread the gospel online. Digital platforms offer unprecedented reach, allowing believers to share the message of Christ with a global audience.

However, this opportunity comes with challenges such as digital noise, short attention spans, and the potential for misunderstandings in a text-based medium. Effective digital evangelism requires creativity and adaptability, utilizing various forms of content—such as videos, blogs, podcasts, and social media posts—to communicate the gospel in engaging and relatable ways.

It also involves building genuine relationships and communities online, where meaningful conversations about faith can take place. Christians must be prepared to answer questions, provide support, and demonstrate the love of Christ through their interactions. While the digital landscape can be daunting, it also offers immense potential for reaching those who may never step into a church. By approaching digital evangelism with prayerful consideration and strategic planning, believers can harness the power of technology to share the transformative message of the gospel.

In summary, Christian behavior in the digital age involves navigating social media and online interactions with discernment and grace, maintaining integrity and witness in all digital engagements, and embracing the challenges and opportunities of digital evangelism. By doing so, Christians can extend their faith into the digital realm, creating a positive impact and reaching a broader audience with the message of Christ. Through thoughtful and intentional engagement, believers can reflect the love, truth, and grace of God in every corner of the digital world, drawing others toward the hope and salvation found in Jesus.

Christian behavior, while rooted in faith and guided by biblical principles, is not immune to challenges. Believers often face temptations and trials that test their commitment to living according to God's will. Overcoming these challenges requires perseverance and faithfulness, as well as strong support systems composed of church, family, and friends.

Temptations and trials are inevitable in the Christian journey. Temptation, as described in James 1:14, comes when we are enticed by our own desires. These desires can lead us away from God's path, causing us to stumble in our behavior. Trials, on the other hand, are external difficulties and hardships that test our faith and resilience. Both temptations and trials can be formidable obstacles to maintaining Christian behavior, but they also present opportunities for growth and strengthening of faith. Overcoming temptation involves recognizing its source, resisting the urge to give in, and relying on God's strength and guidance. This requires a deep understanding of Scripture, which equips believers with the truth needed to counteract lies and deceptions. Trials, while challenging, can refine our character and deepen our dependence on God. By facing these difficulties with a trusting heart, believers can emerge stronger and more committed to their faith.

Perseverance and faithfulness are essential qualities for overcoming the challenges to Christian behavior. Perseverance involves steadfastly enduring difficulties and remaining committed to God's commandments, even when the path is hard. It is about continuing in faith despite setbacks, doubts, or failures.

Faithfulness is closely related, emphasizing a consistent and unwavering commitment to God and His teachings. Hebrews 12:1-2 encourages believers to "run with perseverance the race marked out for us, fixing our eyes on Jesus, the pioneer and perfecter of faith." This passage highlights the importance of staying focused on Christ, drawing strength from His example and the promises of God. Practically, perseverance and faithfulness are cultivated through regular spiritual disciplines such as prayer, Bible study, and worship. These practices fortify believers against the pressures and temptations of the world, enabling them to remain true to their Christian values.

Support systems are vital for overcoming challenges to Christian behavior. The church, family, and friends provide the encouragement, accountability, and companionship needed to navigate life's difficulties.

The church is a community of believers who gather to worship, learn, and support one another. It offers a space for mutual encouragement and spiritual growth through teaching, fellowship, and collective prayer. Family, particularly within the context of a Christian household, provides a foundational support system where faith is nurtured and lived out daily. Parents, spouses, and children can encourage one another, offer guidance, and model Christian behavior. Friends who share the same faith can be a source of strength and accountability, helping each other stay on the right path and offering comfort in times of need. Engaging with these support systems helps believers remain connected to a larger body of Christ, providing the relational support necessary to overcome challenges.

TRUE PRINCIPLES OF CHRISTIANITY BOOK TWO

Overcoming challenges to Christian behavior involves addressing temptations and trials with a resolute faith, cultivating perseverance and faithfulness, and relying on support systems like the church, family, and friends. By recognizing and resisting temptation, enduring trials with trust in God, and drawing strength from supportive relationships, believers can maintain their commitment to living according to God's will. These elements work together to fortify Christians against the pressures and difficulties they face, enabling them to live out their faith with integrity and resilience. Through the collective strength of perseverance, faithfulness, and community support, believers can navigate the challenges of life, growing stronger in their faith and more effective in their witness to the world.

In conclusion, Christian behavior is a comprehensive reflection of one's faith, encompassing every aspect of life, from personal integrity and interpersonal relationships to social and cultural engagement and digital interactions. Rooted in the biblical mandate to live holy and upright lives, believers are called to embody the character of Christ in all they do. This involves understanding and practicing the Fruit of the Spirit, adhering to ethical principles, engaging constructively with society and culture, and maintaining a consistent witness in the digital age.

Living a Christ-centered life means continually striving to align one's actions and attitudes with the teachings of Jesus. It requires an ongoing commitment to love and forgive, serve humbly, resolve conflicts, and reconcile relationships. Believers must navigate the challenges of temptations and trials with perseverance and faithfulness, supported by the church, family, and friends. Social media and other digital platforms present unique opportunities and challenges, demanding discernment and integrity to maintain a positive and godly influence.

As you reflect on these key points, I encourage you to embrace the call to live a Christ-centered life. Let your behavior in every area of life be a testament to the transformative power of the gospel. Strive to embody the love, joy, peace, patience, kindness, goodness, faithfulness, gentleness, and self-control that the Holy Spirit cultivates within you. Seek to influence your community and the broader society with the values of the kingdom of God, always maintaining your spiritual integrity.

May you find strength and encouragement in the knowledge that you are not alone in this journey. The Holy Spirit is your guide and helper, empowering you to live out your faith. Lean on the support of your church, family, and friends as you navigate the challenges and opportunities of life.

Let us pray. Heavenly Father, we thank You for Your unfailing love and grace. We come before You, acknowledging our need for Your strength and guidance in our daily conduct. Help us to live lives that reflect the character of Christ in all we do. Grant us wisdom and discernment as we navigate the complexities of this world, especially in our online interactions. Strengthen us to resist temptations and endure trials with faithfulness. Surround us with supportive relationships that encourage and uplift us. Empower us by Your Holy Spirit to bear the Fruit of the Spirit, so that our lives may be a testament to Your transforming power. May our words and actions always bring glory to Your name and draw others to the hope we have in You. In Jesus' name, we pray. Amen.

9. Marriage and Family

Marriage and family hold a profound significance in human society, serving as the bedrock of social stability and personal fulfillment. At its core, marriage is a lifelong covenant between a man and a woman, established by mutual commitment and love, and grounded in the principles of fidelity, partnership, and mutual support. The family, formed through the union of marriage, is the primary institution for nurturing and developing individuals, providing a context for emotional security, moral instruction, and socialization. It is within the family that values are transmitted, character is shaped, and faith is cultivated.

The importance of marriage and family is deeply rooted in the biblical narrative. From the very beginning, the Bible presents marriage as a divine institution, established by God Himself. In the book of Genesis, we see the creation of the first human beings, Adam and Eve, and their union in marriage as a fundamental aspect of God's design for humanity. "Therefore a man shall leave his father and mother and be joined to his wife, and they shall become one flesh" (Genesis 2:24). This foundational verse underscores the permanence and intimacy intended for marriage.

Furthermore, the Bible portrays marriage as a reflection of the relationship between Christ and the Church. The Apostle Paul, in his letter to the Ephesians, writes, "Husbands, love your wives, just as Christ also loved the church and gave Himself for her" (Ephesians 5:25). This profound analogy elevates the marital relationship to a sacred level, illustrating the selfless love and sacrificial commitment that should characterize Christian marriages.

The purpose of this chapter is to explore the biblical principles and practical aspects of marriage and family, offering guidance and encouragement to individuals and couples seeking to build strong, healthy, and God-honoring relationships. We will delve into the roles and responsibilities of husbands and wives, the vital role of the family in God's plan, and the ways in which marriage serves as a reflection of Christ's relationship with the Church. Additionally, we will address common challenges faced in marriage, providing biblical solutions and practical advice for overcoming them.

By examining the principles laid out in Scripture and considering their application in contemporary contexts, this chapter aims to equip readers with the knowledge and tools necessary to cultivate thriving marriages and families. In doing so, we hope to foster a deeper understanding of the divine purpose for these institutions and inspire a renewed commitment to living out God's design for marriage and family in everyday life.

The biblical view of marriage is deeply rooted in the narrative of creation, where God Himself instituted the union between man and woman. According to Genesis, marriage is not a human invention but a divine ordinance established at the very beginning of human history. God created man and woman in His own image, and He saw that it was not good for man to be alone. Thus, He created Eve as a suitable helper for Adam, bringing her to him and establishing the first marriage. This act is foundational, highlighting that marriage is God's design for companionship, mutual support, and procreation.

In Genesis 2:24, we read, "Therefore a man shall leave his father and mother and be joined to his wife, and they shall become one flesh." This passage underscores the divine institution of marriage, indicating that it is a sacred covenant. Unlike a mere contract, which can be broken, a covenant is a solemn and binding agreement made before God. It involves a lifelong commitment and embodies the principles of loyalty, faithfulness, and unconditional love. In marriage, the covenantal nature is reflected in the vows exchanged, signifying a pledge to remain united through all circumstances.

The roles and responsibilities of husbands and wives in a biblical marriage are clearly defined in Scripture, providing a framework for a harmonious and fulfilling partnership. Husbands are called to exercise headship, not as domineering rulers, but as loving leaders who model their role after Christ's sacrificial love for the Church. Ephesians 5:25 instructs, "Husbands, love your wives, just as Christ also loved the church and gave Himself for her." This love is characterized by selflessness, service, and a willingness to prioritize the wife's well-being above one's own desires.

Wives, in turn, are called to submit to their husbands' leadership, as unto the Lord. This submission is not about inferiority or blind obedience, but about recognizing and respecting the God-given role of the husband as the head of the household. Ephesians 5:22-23 states, "Wives, submit to your own husbands, as to the Lord. For the husband is head of the wife, as also Christ is head of the church; and He is the Savior of the body." Submission, in this context, is an act of trust and partnership, allowing the husband to lead while maintaining mutual respect and dignity.

The biblical view of marriage also emphasizes mutual love and respect between spouses. Ephesians 5:33 encapsulates this dynamic: "Nevertheless let each one of you in particular so love his own wife as himself, and let the wife see that she respects her husband." Love and respect are the twin pillars that sustain a healthy marriage. For husbands, this means cherishing their wives, honoring them, and nurturing them with tender care. For wives, it means valuing their husbands, supporting their leadership, and affirming their efforts.

In summary, the biblical view of marriage presents it as a divine institution, a sacred covenant reflecting God's design and purpose. It outlines distinct yet complementary roles for husbands and wives, with headship and submission framed within the context of Christ-like love and mutual respect. This model, when embraced, fosters unity, strength, and a deep sense of fulfillment, enabling couples to experience the fullness of God's blessing in their marital relationship.

The family holds a central place in God's plan, serving as the foundational unit of society and the primary context for spiritual nurture and character development. In God's design, the family is more than just a social construct; it is an institution ordained by Him to fulfill specific purposes that are essential for individual growth, community stability, and the transmission of faith and values across generations.

As the basic unit of society, the family is where individuals first learn to relate to others and understand their roles within a community. The family provides a structure in which members can experience love, security, and belonging. Within this setting, children are taught the principles of social interaction, respect for authority, and the importance of contributing to the welfare of others. The stability and strength of society are directly linked to the health and vitality of its families. Strong families contribute to social cohesion, economic productivity, and the overall well-being of communities. Conversely, the breakdown of the family unit often leads to social fragmentation, increased crime, and other societal issues.

The family is also the primary environment for spiritual nurture. According to the Bible, parents have the responsibility to teach their children about God, His commandments, and His love. In Deuteronomy 6:6-7, we read, "And these words which I command you today shall be in your heart. You shall teach them diligently to your children, and shall talk of them when you sit in your house, when you walk by the way, when you lie down, and when you rise up." This passage highlights the continuous and intentional effort required in spiritual instruction, encompassing all aspects of daily life. Through prayer, Bible study, and modeling a Christ-like character, parents can cultivate a strong foundation of faith in their children, guiding them towards a personal relationship with God.

Character development is another critical role of the family in God's plan. It is within the family that individuals first learn moral values, ethical behavior, and the virtues of honesty, kindness, patience, and self-discipline. Parents are tasked with the responsibility of shaping their children's character through discipline, instruction, and example. Proverbs 22:6 advises, "Train up a child in the way he should go, and when he is old he will not depart from it." This training involves setting boundaries, enforcing consequences, and providing encouragement and guidance to help children develop into responsible and morally upright adults. The family environment, with its unique blend of love and authority, is ideally suited for this formative process.

Moreover, the family plays a vital role in preparing individuals for broader societal engagement. By teaching children to honor commitments, work diligently, and respect others, families contribute to the development of good citizens and effective leaders. The virtues and values instilled within the family extend beyond its boundaries, influencing schools, workplaces, and communities.

In summary, the family occupies a pivotal role in God's plan, functioning as the basic unit of society, the primary environment for spiritual nurture, and the principal context for character development. Through the family, God intends to create a stable, nurturing, and morally sound foundation for individuals, which in turn strengthens society and advances His kingdom on earth. By fulfilling these roles, families can reflect God's love and wisdom, contributing to the flourishing of both individuals and communities.

Marriage, in its biblical conception, is profoundly symbolic, reflecting the deep and mysterious relationship between Christ and His Church. This divine analogy elevates the marital bond to a sacred level, illustrating profound truths about God's love, commitment, and covenant with His people. Through this symbolism, the roles of husbands and wives are given a theological foundation that underscores their mutual responsibilities and privileges within the marriage covenant.

The symbolism of marriage as a reflection of Christ and the Church is rooted in the Apostle Paul's teachings in the New Testament. In Ephesians 5:31-32, Paul writes, "For this reason a man shall leave his father and mother and be joined to his wife, and the two shall become one flesh. This is a great mystery, but I speak concerning Christ and the church." Here, Paul reveals that the union of husband and wife is a living illustration of the spiritual union between Christ and the Church. Just as a husband and wife become one flesh in marriage, Christ and the Church are united in a profound spiritual bond. This union is characterized by intimacy, love, and mutual commitment, reflecting the ultimate relationship between the divine and humanity.

Christ's love for the Church serves as the model for husbands in their role within the marriage. Ephesians 5:25-27 states, "Husbands, love your wives, just as Christ also loved the church and gave Himself for her, that He might sanctify and cleanse her with the washing of water by the word, that He might present her to Himself a glorious church, not having spot or wrinkle or any such thing, but that she should be holy and without blemish."

This passage emphasizes the self-sacrificial nature of Christ's love, which is the standard for husbands. Just as Christ gave Himself up for the Church, husbands are called to love their wives with a selfless, sacrificial love that seeks their well-being and spiritual growth. This love is not conditional or self-serving but is characterized by humility, service, and an unwavering commitment to the wife's welfare.

The Church's response to Christ provides the model for wives in their role within the marriage. Ephesians 5:22-24 instructs, "Wives, submit to your own husbands, as to the Lord. For the husband is head of the wife, as also Christ is head of the church; and He is the Savior of the body.

Therefore, just as the church is subject to Christ, so let the wives be to their own husbands in everything." This submission is not about subjugation or inferiority but about respect, trust, and the willingness to support the husband's leadership. It mirrors the Church's relationship with Christ, characterized by reverence, cooperation, and a shared mission. In this context, submission is an act of partnership, recognizing the husband's role while maintaining equality and mutual respect.

The marriage relationship, therefore, becomes a tangible expression of the gospel, illustrating the depth of Christ's love and the Church's devotion. When husbands and wives embrace these roles, their marriage becomes a living testimony to God's redemptive plan and His covenantal relationship with His people. This divine pattern promotes a harmonious and fulfilling partnership, where both spouses thrive in their God-given roles, supporting and nurturing each other in love and respect.

In summary, marriage as a reflection of Christ and the Church imbues the marital relationship with profound spiritual significance. The symbolism of marriage illustrates the intimate and sacrificial love of Christ for the Church and the respectful and supportive response of the Church to Christ. By embodying these principles, husbands and wives can experience the fullness of God's design for marriage, creating a union that honors God and enriches their lives together.

Christian marriages, like all marriages, face a variety of challenges that can test the strength and unity of the relationship. However, with a foundation rooted in biblical principles, couples can navigate these difficulties and build a resilient, fulfilling partnership. Key areas where challenges often arise include communication and conflict resolution, financial management and stewardship, intimacy and sexuality, and maintaining a Christ-centered marriage.

Effective communication and conflict resolution are essential for a healthy marriage. Misunderstandings, differing perspectives, and unmet expectations can lead to conflicts, but how couples address these issues determines the health of their relationship. Ephesians 4:29 advises, "Let no corrupt word proceed out of your mouth, but what is good for necessary edification, that it may impart grace to the hearers." Couples should strive to communicate with kindness, honesty, and respect, focusing on building each other up rather than tearing each other down. When conflicts arise, it is important to address them promptly and constructively. Matthew 18:15-17 provides a model for resolving disputes, emphasizing direct and honest communication aimed at reconciliation. By practicing active listening, empathy, and forgiveness, couples can overcome conflicts and strengthen their bond.

Financial management and stewardship are also critical aspects of a successful marriage. Money issues are a common source of stress and conflict, but approaching finances with a biblical mindset can help couples navigate these challenges. Proverbs 22:7 warns, "The rich rules over the poor, and the borrower is servant to the lender."

Couples should work together to create a budget, live within their means, and avoid unnecessary debt. Stewardship involves recognizing that all resources belong to God and managing them wisely. This includes tithing, saving, and making financial decisions that honor God and reflect a commitment to generosity. Open and honest discussions about finances, shared goals, and a unified approach to managing money can prevent financial stress and foster a sense of teamwork and trust.

Intimacy and sexuality are vital components of a healthy marriage, yet they can also be areas of difficulty. The Bible celebrates sexual intimacy within marriage as a gift from God, intended for pleasure, procreation, and the deepening of the marital bond. 1 Corinthians 7:3-5 emphasizes the importance of mutual fulfillment and consent in sexual relationships. Couples should prioritize intimacy, recognizing its role in strengthening their connection.

This involves open communication about needs and desires, as well as addressing any issues that may arise, such as physical or emotional barriers to intimacy. Maintaining a healthy sexual relationship requires intentional effort, sensitivity, and a commitment to meeting each other's needs.

Maintaining a Christ-centered marriage is perhaps the most crucial aspect of overcoming challenges and building a lasting union. A marriage centered on Christ provides a solid foundation that can withstand trials and difficulties. Couples should prioritize their spiritual growth both individually and together. This includes regular prayer, Bible study, and involvement in a faith community. Colossians 3:16 encourages believers to "let the word of Christ dwell in you richly in all wisdom, teaching and admonishing one another in psalms and hymns and spiritual songs, singing with grace in your hearts to the Lord." By keeping Christ at the center, couples can draw strength, wisdom, and guidance from their faith, enabling them to navigate challenges with grace and resilience.

In conclusion, while Christian marriages face a variety of challenges, these can be effectively addressed through biblical principles and practical solutions. Effective communication and conflict resolution, wise financial management and stewardship, healthy intimacy and sexuality, and maintaining a Christ-centered focus are key elements in building a strong, resilient marriage. By embracing these principles, couples can overcome difficulties and experience the fullness of God's design for their union, creating a partnership that glorifies God and enriches their lives.

Parenting and raising godly children is a profound responsibility and privilege entrusted to parents by God. The Bible provides clear principles and guidance on how to nurture and instruct children in a manner that honors God and fosters their spiritual growth. By adhering to these biblical principles, parents can cultivate an environment that promotes the development of godly character and faith in their children.

The Bible outlines several fundamental principles for parenting that emphasize the importance of love, guidance, and instruction. Ephesians 6:4 advises, "And you, fathers, do not provoke your children to wrath, but bring them up in the training and admonition of the Lord." This verse highlights the need for parents to create a nurturing and supportive environment, avoiding harshness or unreasonable demands that can lead to resentment. Instead, parents are called to raise their children with consistent, loving guidance rooted in biblical truth. The principles of patience, kindness, and unconditional love should permeate all aspects of parenting, reflecting the character of God.

Discipline and instruction play a crucial role in the upbringing of godly children. Proverbs 22:6 emphasizes the importance of early training: "Train up a child in the way he should go, and when he is old he will not depart from it."

Discipline, when administered with love and consistency, helps children understand boundaries and develop self-control. It is essential for parents to establish clear expectations and consequences, teaching their children the difference between right and wrong. However, discipline should always be balanced with instruction, offering guidance and encouragement. Proverbs 13:24 states, "He who spares his rod hates his son, but he who loves him disciplines him promptly." This underscores that loving discipline is an expression of care and concern for the child's well-being and future.

Encouraging spiritual growth in children involves more than just teaching them about God; it requires creating an environment where faith can flourish. Deuteronomy 6:6-7 instructs parents to diligently teach their children God's commandments and to integrate spiritual discussions into everyday life: "And these words which I command you today shall be in your heart. You shall teach them diligently to your children, and shall talk of them when you sit in your house, when you walk by the way, when you lie down, and when you rise up."

Regular family devotions, prayer, and participation in a faith community are vital practices that help children develop a personal relationship with God. Encouraging children to ask questions, express their faith, and participate in spiritual activities fosters a deeper understanding and commitment to their faith.

The influence of parental example cannot be overstated. Children learn not only through instruction but also by observing their parents' actions and attitudes. Proverbs 20:7 states, "The righteous man walks in his integrity; his children are blessed after him." Parents who model godly behavior, integrity, and faithfulness provide a powerful testimony to their children. Living out one's faith in everyday situations—showing kindness, forgiveness, humility, and a genuine love for God—creates a lasting impact on children. It is through this consistent example that children learn to internalize and practice the values and principles of their faith.

In conclusion, parenting and raising godly children is a multifaceted task that requires love, discipline, instruction, encouragement, and the power of a godly example. By adhering to biblical principles, parents can create a nurturing environment that promotes spiritual growth and character development. Through loving discipline, consistent instruction, and a strong personal example, parents can guide their children towards a deep, abiding faith and a life that honors God. This sacred responsibility, when undertaken with prayer and reliance on God's wisdom, can lead to the flourishing of godly generations who will continue to uphold and spread the values of their faith.

The extended family and the church community play vital roles in providing support, nurture, and spiritual growth. These broader networks offer additional resources, wisdom, and encouragement that can significantly enhance the well-being and development of individuals and families. By embracing the extended family and church community, families can experience a deeper sense of belonging, intergenerational connections, and mentorship that enrich their lives and faith journeys.

The role of the extended family in support and nurture is a crucial aspect of God's design for familial relationships. Extended family members, such as grandparents, aunts, uncles, and cousins, provide an additional layer of love, care, and guidance.

They often contribute unique perspectives and experiences that can help children and parents navigate life's challenges. In the Bible, we see examples of extended families playing important roles, such as Naomi and Ruth, where familial bonds extend beyond the immediate nuclear family. Extended family members can offer practical support, such as childcare, financial assistance, and emotional encouragement, fostering a sense of stability and security. Proverbs 17:6 highlights the value of these relationships: "Children's children are a crown to the aged, and parents are the pride of their children."

The church as a family is a powerful metaphor that underscores the spiritual and communal bonds among believers. The New Testament frequently refers to the church as the body of Christ, with each member playing a vital role in its functioning and well-being. Ephesians 2:19-22 speaks to this unity: "Consequently, you are no longer foreigners and strangers, but fellow citizens with God's people and also members of his household, built on the foundation of the apostles and prophets, with Christ Jesus himself as the chief cornerstone."

The church community provides spiritual nurture, accountability, and a sense of belonging that complements and extends the support of the nuclear and extended family. Through corporate worship, communal prayer, and shared experiences, church members can grow in their faith and support each other in their spiritual journeys.

Intergenerational relationships and mentoring are essential components of a healthy church community and extended family.

These relationships allow for the transmission of wisdom, values, and traditions from one generation to the next. Titus 2:3-5 encourages older women to mentor younger women, teaching them to live godly lives and fulfill their roles with wisdom and grace. Similarly, older men are called to set an example for younger men in faith and conduct. These mentoring relationships provide opportunities for personal growth, spiritual development, and practical guidance. Intergenerational connections also help bridge generational gaps, fostering mutual understanding and respect.

In a church community, mentoring can take various forms, including formal discipleship programs, small group gatherings, and informal relationships. By investing in the next generation, older church members can leave a lasting legacy of faith and service. Younger members, in turn, can benefit from the experience and insights of those who have walked the path of faith before them. This dynamic creates a vibrant, supportive, and spiritually rich environment where all members can flourish.

The extended family and church community are integral to providing support, nurture, and spiritual growth for individuals and families. The extended family offers additional layers of care and guidance, enriching the lives of children and parents. The church community, viewed as a family, provides spiritual nurture, accountability, and a sense of belonging that complements the support of the nuclear and extended family. Intergenerational relationships and mentoring within the church and family context enable the transmission of wisdom, values, and faith, fostering mutual growth and understanding. By embracing these broader networks, families can experience a deeper sense of community and spiritual enrichment, fulfilling God's design for relational and communal support.

In contemporary society, marriage and family dynamics face numerous challenges and complexities that require thoughtful and compassionate responses rooted in biblical principles. Issues such as divorce and remarriage, single parenthood and blended families, cultural and societal changes, and the influence of the digital age all impact the stability and health of families. Addressing these modern issues involves a balance of grace, truth, and practical support, ensuring that families can thrive despite these challenges.

Divorce and remarriage present significant challenges within the context of Christian marriage. The Bible emphasizes the sanctity and permanence of marriage, as seen in Matthew 19:6: "So they are no longer two, but one flesh.

Therefore, what God has joined together, let no one separate." However, the reality of broken relationships and the pain of divorce cannot be ignored. While divorce is not God's ideal, it is sometimes necessary due to circumstances such as infidelity, abuse, or abandonment. The church must offer support and healing for those who have experienced divorce, providing counseling and community to help individuals rebuild their lives. Regarding remarriage, pastoral guidance is crucial to navigate the complexities of individual situations, ensuring that decisions honor God's intentions for marriage and family while offering grace and redemption.

Single parenthood and blended families are increasingly common in modern society, presenting unique challenges and opportunities for growth. Single parents often face significant burdens, including financial strain, emotional stress, and the challenge of raising children alone.

The church and extended family can play a vital role in supporting single parents, offering practical assistance, emotional encouragement, and spiritual guidance. Blended families, which arise from remarriage, must navigate the complexities of integrating different family cultures, establishing new relationships, and managing co-parenting arrangements. Open communication, mutual respect, and a commitment to unity are essential for blended families to thrive. The church can support these families by providing resources, counseling, and opportunities for community building.

Cultural and societal changes continue to influence the dynamics of marriage and family. Issues such as shifting gender roles, changing societal norms, and diverse family structures require Christians to engage with cultural trends thoughtfully and biblically. Romans 12:2 advises, "Do not conform to the pattern of this world, but be transformed by the renewing of your mind." Christians are called to uphold biblical values while engaging with the world in a way that is loving and respectful. This involves understanding the cultural context, addressing societal pressures, and providing a countercultural witness that reflects God's design for marriage and family. By grounding their lives in Scripture and seeking God's wisdom, families can navigate cultural changes without compromising their faith.

Promoting healthy relationships in a digital age is another pressing issue for modern families. The proliferation of digital technology, social media, and online communication has transformed how people interact, often leading to increased screen time, diminished face-to-face interactions, and the potential for unhealthy relationships. Families must be intentional about setting boundaries for technology use, prioritizing quality time together, and fostering meaningful connections.

Ephesians 5:15-16 advises, "Be very careful, then, how you live—not as unwise but as wise, making the most of every opportunity, because the days are evil." By establishing guidelines for technology use and encouraging activities that promote real-life engagement and connection, families can mitigate the negative impacts of the digital age.

Addressing modern issues in marriage and family requires a balanced approach that incorporates biblical principles, practical support, and compassionate understanding. Divorce and remarriage, single parenthood and blended families, cultural and societal changes, and the influence of the digital age all present challenges that can be navigated with God's wisdom and guidance. By fostering supportive communities, providing resources and counseling, and promoting healthy, Christ-centered relationships, families can thrive despite the complexities of contemporary life. Through reliance on God's grace and a commitment to biblical values, families can overcome these challenges and experience the fullness of His design for marriage and family.

In conclusion, the journey of exploring marriage and family through a biblical lens reveals the profound significance and purpose these institutions hold in God's design. Throughout this chapter, we have delved into various aspects of marriage and family, uncovering key principles and practical applications that underscore their importance in the Christian faith.

We began by defining marriage and family and highlighting their biblical foundation. Marriage, instituted by God at creation, is a sacred covenant that mirrors Christ's relationship with the Church. The roles and responsibilities of husbands and wives, rooted in love, respect, and mutual submission, provide a framework for a harmonious and fulfilling union. The family, as the basic unit of society, plays a crucial role in spiritual nurture and character development, fostering an environment where faith and values are cultivated and passed down through generations.

We also examined the challenges that modern marriages and families face, such as communication and conflict resolution, financial management, intimacy, and maintaining a Christ-centered focus. By adhering to biblical principles and seeking God's guidance, couples can navigate these challenges and build resilient, thriving relationships. Furthermore, the role of extended family and the church community in providing support, mentorship, and intergenerational connections highlights the collective responsibility in nurturing and sustaining strong families.

TRUE PRINCIPLES OF CHRISTIANITY BOOK TWO

In addressing contemporary issues like divorce, remarriage, single parenthood, blended families, cultural changes, and the influence of the digital age, we emphasized the need for a compassionate and balanced approach. By grounding our responses in Scripture and offering practical support, the faith community can help families overcome these challenges and experience healing and growth.

As we conclude this chapter, it is essential to offer encouragement and hope for Christian families. Despite the complexities and difficulties that may arise, there is hope in God's promises and His unwavering love. Ephesians 3:20 reminds us that God is able to do "immeasurably more than all we ask or imagine, according to his power that is at work within us." With God's help, families can overcome obstacles, grow in faith, and experience the joy and fulfillment that He intends for them.

Strong marriages and families are vital to the health and vibrancy of the faith community. They serve as a testament to God's love and faithfulness, providing a living example of His grace and truth. By nurturing healthy relationships, fostering spiritual growth, and supporting one another, the faith community can create an environment where families flourish and God's kingdom is advanced.

In the end, the importance of strong marriages and families cannot be overstated. They are the foundation upon which individuals and communities are built, reflecting God's design and purpose. As we continue to seek His guidance and rely on His strength, we can uphold and celebrate the beauty and significance of marriage and family, honoring God and impacting the world around us. Through dedication, love, and a commitment to biblical principles, Christian families can thrive and contribute to a legacy of faith that endures for generations.

10. Christ's Ultimate Ministry

The doctrine of Christ's ministry in the Heavenly Sanctuary is a central tenet of Christian theology that illuminates the profound work Jesus continues to perform on behalf of humanity. Understanding this doctrine is crucial for grasping the full scope of Christ's redemptive mission and its ongoing implications for believers. This doctrine is rooted in the biblical portrayal of Jesus as our High Priest, who, after His ascension, entered the heavenly sanctuary to intercede for us and complete the work of salvation.

The concept of the heavenly sanctuary finds its foundations in the typology of the Old Testament sanctuary services, which were instituted by God to illustrate the steps in His plan of salvation. The earthly sanctuary, with its intricate design and sacrificial system, served as a symbolic representation of the heavenly realities. It was a tangible expression of God's desire to dwell among His people and to provide a means of reconciliation and atonement for sin. In the New Testament, particularly in the book of Hebrews, we find that these earthly symbols are fulfilled and surpassed by the true ministry of Christ in the heavenly sanctuary.

Christ's ascension to heaven marked the beginning of His intercessory work as our High Priest. Unlike the priests of the Old Testament, who repeatedly offered sacrifices, Jesus offered Himself once for all as the perfect sacrifice. Now, in the heavenly sanctuary, He presents His own blood before the Father, interceding on behalf of believers. This ongoing ministry is essential for our understanding of salvation, as it assures us that Christ's atoning sacrifice on the cross is continually applied to our lives, granting us forgiveness and grace.

One of the key aspects of Christ's heavenly ministry is His role in the investigative judgment and the cleansing of the sanctuary. This concept, derived from the prophecy of Daniel, reveals that before the final consummation of all things, there is a phase of judgment in which the records of humanity are examined. Christ, as our advocate, examines these records, ensuring that those who have placed their faith in Him are vindicated. The cleansing of the heavenly sanctuary signifies the removal of sin from the universe and the restoration of perfect harmony between God and His creation.

Understanding Christ's ministry in the heavenly sanctuary deepens our appreciation of His love and commitment to humanity. It provides believers with assurance and confidence, knowing that Jesus is actively working on their behalf, applying the merits of His sacrifice, and preparing a place for them in His eternal kingdom. This doctrine encourages Christians to live lives of faith, repentance, and holiness, fully aware of the heavenly realities that impact their daily existence.

In summary, the study of Christ's ministry in the heavenly sanctuary offers a profound insight into the ongoing work of Jesus as our High Priest. It underscores the continuity and completeness of God's plan of salvation, from the sacrifices of the Old Testament to the ultimate sacrifice of Christ and His continuing intercession. For believers, this understanding is not only theologically enriching but also practically empowering, providing a foundation for a vibrant and assured Christian faith.

The sanctuary holds a central place in biblical theology, embodying both the presence of God among His people and His overarching plan for their salvation. Its purpose and importance are multifaceted, extending from the tangible structures of the Old Testament to the spiritual realities they represent in the New Testament. Understanding the sanctuary is crucial for grasping the depth of God's commitment to humanity and the meticulous care with which He orchestrates the redemption of His creation.

In the Old Testament, the sanctuary, first constructed as the Tabernacle during the Israelites' wilderness journey and later as the Temple in Jerusalem, was the physical location where God chose to dwell among His people. It was a sacred space, meticulously designed according to divine instructions, signifying God's holiness and the need for purity and reverence in approaching Him. The sanctuary was not merely a building; it was the epicenter of Israelite worship and the focal point of God's interaction with His chosen people. It represented a bridge between the divine and the human, where heaven and earth intersected.

The sanctuary's significance is profoundly theological. It illustrated the concept of atonement through its system of sacrifices and offerings. Each aspect of the sanctuary service, from the daily sacrifices to the annual Day of Atonement, was a vivid demonstration of the seriousness of sin and the means by which it could be forgiven. The blood of sacrificial animals, though unable to truly remove sin, symbolized the necessity of a perfect sacrifice to atone for humanity's transgressions. This system pointed forward to the ultimate sacrifice of Jesus Christ, who would offer Himself as the Lamb of God, taking away the sin of the world.

The sanctuary also served as a microcosm of God's plan for salvation. Its structure and services were a shadow of heavenly realities, teaching vital spiritual truths about God's character and His redemptive work. The division of the sanctuary into the Holy Place and the Most Holy Place, along with the specific furnishings and rituals, depicted the steps in the process of salvation—from justification and sanctification to glorification. Each ritual, each piece of furniture, from the altar of burnt offering to the Ark of the Covenant, carried profound symbolic meanings related to the believer's journey from sin to redemption.

In the New Testament, the sanctuary imagery reaches its fulfillment in Christ and His ministry. Jesus is portrayed as the true High Priest who, after offering Himself as the perfect sacrifice, enters the heavenly sanctuary to intercede for His people. The book of Hebrews elucidates this transition, showing that the earthly sanctuary was but a copy and shadow of the heavenly one. Christ's ascension and His ongoing work in the heavenly sanctuary assure believers that the work of redemption continues. His presence in the heavenly sanctuary confirms that God's plan for salvation is not only comprehensive but also dynamic, continually applying the benefits of His atoning sacrifice to those who believe.

Thus, the sanctuary is a reflection of God's plan for salvation, a divine blueprint revealing how He deals with sin and reconciles humanity to Himself. It underscores God's desire to dwell with His people, His holiness, and the necessity of atonement. Moreover, it highlights the continuity of God's redemptive work from the Old Testament to the New Testament, culminating in the ministry of Christ in the heavenly sanctuary. This understanding enriches the believer's faith, providing assurance that God's plan is both perfect and ongoing, rooted in His unchanging character and boundless love.

In summary, the sanctuary in biblical theology is a profound testament to God's meticulous and loving plan for human redemption. Its purpose and importance transcend its physical manifestations, pointing to the spiritual realities of salvation through Christ. By studying the sanctuary, believers gain deeper insights into God's holiness, the gravity of sin, and the immeasurable grace extended through Jesus's sacrificial death and ongoing intercession. This understanding not only deepens theological knowledge but also fortifies faith, offering a robust foundation for a life devoted to God.

The earthly sanctuary, as described in Exodus 25-27, was a meticulously designed structure that served as the dwelling place of God among the Israelites. It was a portable tent known as the

Tabernacle, which was later succeeded by the more permanent Temple in Jerusalem. Both structures followed a divinely revealed blueprint, rich in symbolic meaning, representing various aspects of God's plan for salvation and His relationship with His people.

The Tabernacle was divided into three main sections: the Outer Court, the Holy Place, and the Most Holy Place. Each section had specific furnishings and served distinct purposes, reflecting the journey from sin to communion with God.

The Outer Court was the first area encountered upon entering the sanctuary grounds. It contained the Altar of Burnt Offering and the Laver. The Altar of Burnt Offering was where the priests offered sacrifices for the atonement of sin. This altar symbolized the need for a sacrificial atonement to reconcile humanity with God, prefiguring Christ's ultimate sacrifice on the cross. The Laver, a large basin filled with water, was used by the priests for ceremonial washing before entering the Holy Place. This act of washing represented purification and the need for holiness when approaching God.

The Holy Place was the first chamber within the Tabernacle itself, accessible only to the priests. It housed three significant pieces of furniture: the Table of Showbread, the Golden Lampstand, and the Altar of Incense. The Table of Showbread held twelve loaves of bread, symbolizing God's provision and the sustenance He provides to His people. The Golden Lampstand, a seven-branched candelabrum, represented the light of God's presence and His guidance. The Altar of Incense, situated before the veil separating the Holy Place from the Most Holy Place, was used to burn incense, symbolizing the prayers of the saints ascending to God.

The Most Holy Place, or the Holy of Holies, was the innermost and most sacred area of the Tabernacle, entered only once a year by the High Priest on the Day of Atonement. It contained the Ark of the Covenant, a gold-covered wooden chest that held the tablets of the Ten Commandments, a pot of manna, and Aaron's rod that budded.

The Ark was topped with the Mercy Seat, flanked by two cherubim. The Most Holy Place represented the very presence of God, with the Mercy Seat symbolizing His throne of grace and mercy. The Day of Atonement rituals performed here foreshadowed the ultimate atonement brought by Christ.

The design and furnishings of the sanctuary were laden with symbolic meanings that pointed to deeper spiritual truths. The overall layout illustrated the progression from the world outside the sanctuary, through stages of purification and enlightenment, to the intimate presence of God. Each element within the sanctuary had profound theological implications.

The sacrifices at the altar pointed to the need for a perfect, atoning sacrifice. The laver emphasized the importance of spiritual cleansing. The bread and light within the Holy Place symbolized sustenance and divine guidance. The incense altar underscored the power and importance of prayer. Finally, the Ark of the Covenant and the Mercy Seat highlighted the centrality of God's law, His covenant with His people, and His willingness to extend mercy and forgiveness.

The arrangement of the sanctuary thus provided a comprehensive picture of the process of salvation, from justification and sanctification to glorification. It was a tangible representation of God's redemptive plan, teaching the Israelites and future generations about the holiness of God, the gravity of sin, and the means of reconciliation provided by God Himself.

In summary, the appearance and arrangement of the earthly sanctuary were divinely orchestrated to teach profound spiritual truths. The sanctuary's layout and its elements were not only functional but also symbolically rich, each part reflecting different aspects of God's character and His plan for humanity's salvation. By studying the sanctuary, believers gain a deeper appreciation of the meticulous care with which God communicates His love and the path to redemption.

The relationship between the heavenly sanctuary and the earthly sanctuary is foundational to understanding the typology and foreshadowing present in the Bible. The earthly sanctuary, with its rituals and design, served as a shadow and a copy of the true heavenly sanctuary. This typological relationship is explicitly mentioned in Hebrews 8:5, where it is stated that the priests on earth "serve at a sanctuary that is a copy and shadow of what is in heaven." This connection reveals the deeper spiritual realities that the earthly sanctuary was intended to teach and point forward to.

The earthly sanctuary was meticulously designed by God and given to Moses with precise instructions. Every aspect of its structure and services held symbolic meaning that pointed to the heavenly realities and the greater work that would be accomplished by Christ. The sacrifices, the priestly intercessions, and the layout of the sanctuary were all intended to prepare the minds of the Israelites—and subsequently all believers—for the ultimate sacrifice of Jesus and His ongoing ministry in the heavenly sanctuary.

One of the most significant ways the earthly sanctuary points to the heavenly is through the concept of the High Priest. In the earthly sanctuary, the High Priest played a crucial role, particularly on the Day of Atonement, when he entered the Most Holy Place to make atonement for the sins of the people. This role was a foreshadowing of Christ, our true High Priest, who, after His ascension, entered the heavenly sanctuary to offer His own blood as the final and perfect atonement for sin. Hebrews 9:11-12 highlights this by stating that Christ, "having come as a High Priest of the good things to come, entered the greater and more perfect tabernacle, not made with hands, that is, not of this creation."

Despite the clear typological connections, there are significant differences between the earthly and heavenly sanctuaries. The earthly sanctuary was a physical structure made by human hands, a temporal and tangible representation that could be seen and touched. It was subject to decay and destruction, as evidenced by the destruction of both the Tabernacle and the Temple. In contrast, the heavenly sanctuary is not made with human hands and exists in the spiritual realm. It is eternal, perfect, and beyond the limitations of the physical world.

Another difference lies in the sacrificial system. In the earthly sanctuary, sacrifices were made repeatedly, and the blood of animals was used to atone for sins. These sacrifices were insufficient to truly remove sin but served as a temporary covering and a symbol of the greater sacrifice to come. In the heavenly sanctuary, Christ's sacrifice is once for all. His blood is not just a covering but a complete and final atonement that truly removes sin. Hebrews 10:12-14 states, "But this Man, after He had offered one sacrifice for sins forever, sat down at the right hand of God... For by one offering He has perfected forever those who are being sanctified."

Despite these differences, the similarities between the two sanctuaries are profound and significant. Both serve as places where God's presence dwells and where His people can find atonement and reconciliation. The earthly sanctuary's design and services were a detailed reflection of the heavenly sanctuary's greater realities. The layout—with its Outer Court, Holy Place, and Most Holy Place—paralleled the heavenly sanctuary's structure, symbolizing the stages of approaching God and the process of redemption.

The earthly sanctuary's role in teaching and preparing God's people for the coming of Christ and His ultimate sacrifice cannot be overstated. Through its symbols and rituals, it pointed forward to the greater reality of the heavenly sanctuary where Christ, our High Priest, ministers on our behalf. This typological relationship underscores the continuity of God's plan for salvation and the meticulous care with which He prepared humanity for the revelation of His ultimate redemption through Jesus.

The relationship between the heavenly sanctuary and the earthly sanctuary is one of typology and foreshadowing. The earthly sanctuary, with its rituals and design, served as a shadow of the heavenly sanctuary, preparing the way for the greater and more perfect ministry of Christ. Understanding this relationship enriches our comprehension of God's plan for salvation, the significance of Christ's sacrifice, and His ongoing ministry in the heavenly sanctuary. This typological connection not only bridges the Old and New Testaments but also provides believers with a deeper appreciation of the continuity and fulfillment of God's redemptive work.

The Old Testament sacrificial system, detailed in Leviticus 1-7, was a central component of the worship and religious life of the Israelites. It provided a means for them to atone for their sins, seek reconciliation with God, and express gratitude and devotion. This system was divinely instituted and meticulously regulated, serving as a foreshadowing of the ultimate sacrifice of Jesus Christ.

The sacrificial system included various types of offerings, each with specific purposes and rituals. The main categories of sacrifices were the burnt offering, grain offering, peace offering, sin offering, and guilt offering.

The burnt offering, described in Leviticus 1, was a voluntary act of worship, atonement for unintentional sin, and an expression of devotion and commitment to God. The offering involved the complete burning of a male animal without blemish on the altar, symbolizing the worshiper's total surrender to God and the complete removal of sin.

The grain offering, outlined in Leviticus 2, was also a voluntary act, often accompanying the burnt offering. It consisted of fine flour, olive oil, and frankincense, symbolizing the dedication of the fruits of one's labor to God and a recognition of His provision.

The peace offering, detailed in Leviticus 3, was a voluntary act of fellowship and thanksgiving. It involved the sharing of a meal between the worshiper, the priests, and God, symbolizing reconciliation and communion. The fat portions of the animal were burned on the altar, while the remaining meat was consumed by the worshiper and the priests.

The sin offering, described in Leviticus 4, was mandatory for atonement of specific unintentional sins and ritual impurities. The type of animal offered varied depending on the social status of the individual, reflecting the principle that everyone, regardless of their position, needed atonement. The blood of the sin offering was applied to the horns of the altar and sprinkled before the veil, symbolizing the purification of the sinner and the sanctuary itself.

The guilt offering, outlined in Leviticus 5-7, was also mandatory and was required for offenses requiring restitution. This offering involved the sacrifice of a ram and the payment of compensation to the wronged party. It underscored the necessity of making amends for wrongdoing and the restorative justice of God.

Daily sacrifices were integral to the operation of the sanctuary and the continual atonement for the sins of the people. Every day, a lamb was offered in the morning and another in the evening as burnt offerings, symbolizing the constant need for atonement and the perpetual intercession on behalf of the nation (Exodus 29:38-42). These daily sacrifices maintained the relationship between God and Israel, emphasizing the continuous nature of sin and the unceasing need for reconciliation.

The role of the High Priest in the earthly sanctuary was of paramount importance. The High Priest served as the primary mediator between God and the people, performing the most critical and sacred rituals. He was responsible for entering the Most Holy Place on the Day of Atonement, a solemn and significant event described in Leviticus 16. On this day, the High Priest made atonement for the sins of the entire nation, cleansing the sanctuary and the people through the sacrifice of a bull for his own sins and a goat for the sins of the people. The blood of these animals was sprinkled on the Mercy Seat and before the Ark of the Covenant, symbolizing the purification and forgiveness of the people's sins.

The High Priest's duties extended beyond the Day of Atonement. He also oversaw the daily sacrifices, ensured the maintenance of the sanctuary's purity, and instructed the people in the laws of God. His garments, described in Exodus 28, were richly symbolic, representing the dignity and holiness required for his office. The breastplate, with twelve stones representing the twelve tribes of Israel, signified his role in bearing the people before God. The turban with the inscription "Holy to the Lord" underscored the sacredness of his office and his consecration to God.

In summary, the Old Testament sacrificial system was a comprehensive and divinely instituted means for the Israelites to maintain their relationship with God. It addressed various aspects of worship, atonement, and fellowship, pointing forward to the ultimate sacrifice of Jesus Christ. The daily sacrifices highlighted the ongoing need for atonement, while the High Priest's role underscored the necessity of mediation between a holy God and sinful humanity. This sacrificial system, with its rich symbolism and rituals, laid the groundwork for the New Testament revelation of Christ as the true and perfect sacrifice, fulfilling and surpassing the foreshadowed promises of the Old Covenant.

The Day of Atonement, known as Yom Kippur, is described in Leviticus 16 and stands as one of the most solemn and significant observances in the Jewish religious calendar. It was the only day of the year when the High Priest entered the Most Holy Place of the sanctuary to make atonement for the sins of the entire nation of Israel. This day served both a profound symbolic purpose and carried significant prophetic implications, pointing to the ultimate atonement brought by Jesus Christ.

The Day of Atonement took place on the tenth day of the seventh month, Tishri, and was marked by fasting, prayer, and repentance. It was a day of complete rest, set apart for solemn reflection and seeking forgiveness for sins. The central theme of the day was purification, both of the sanctuary and the people, from the defilement caused by sin over the past year.

On this day, the High Priest performed a series of elaborate and sacred rituals, each loaded with deep symbolic meaning. The rituals began with the High Priest bathing and dressing in special garments made of pure white linen, symbolizing purity and holiness. He first offered a bull as a sin offering for himself and his household, recognizing his own need for atonement before interceding for the people. The blood of this bull was taken into the Most Holy Place and sprinkled on the Mercy Seat and before the Ark of the Covenant.

Next, the High Priest cast lots over two goats to determine their roles in the ceremony. One goat was designated as the "Lord's goat" and the other as the "scapegoat" or Azazel. The Lord's goat was sacrificed as a sin offering for the people, and its blood was brought into the Most Holy Place and sprinkled on the Mercy Seat, just as with the bull's blood. This act symbolized the cleansing of the sanctuary from the impurities of the people's sins.

The High Priest then laid his hands on the head of the scapegoat, confessing over it all the iniquities and transgressions of the Israelites. This symbolic transfer of sins to the scapegoat represented the removal of the people's sins from the community. The scapegoat was then led away into the wilderness, bearing the sins of the people to a solitary place, signifying the complete removal and separation of sin from the people.

The rituals of the Day of Atonement culminated in the cleansing of the altar and the holy places of the sanctuary. The entire process highlighted the severity of sin, the necessity of atonement, and the provision of God's grace in cleansing and forgiving His people.

The symbolic meaning of the Day of Atonement is profound. It underscored the holiness of God and the serious consequences of sin, which not only defiled the individual but also the community and the sanctuary itself. The blood of the sacrifices symbolized the life given to atone for sin, pointing to the ultimate sacrifice of Christ. The scapegoat ritual represented the complete removal of sin, foreshadowing the total forgiveness and cleansing made possible through Jesus.

Prophetically, the Day of Atonement pointed forward to the work of Christ as our High Priest and the ultimate sacrifice for sin. In the New Testament, particularly in the book of Hebrews, the fulfillment of the Day of Atonement is seen in Jesus' ministry. Christ, as the true High Priest, entered not the earthly sanctuary but the heavenly one, offering His own blood as the perfect and final atonement for humanity's sins. Hebrews 9:12 states, "He entered once for all into the holy places, not by means of the blood of goats and calves but by means of his own blood, thus securing an eternal redemption."

Moreover, the concept of the investigative judgment, tied to the cleansing of the sanctuary, is seen in Daniel 8:14, where it is prophesied that the sanctuary will be cleansed after 2300 evenings and mornings. This prophetic cleansing is understood by many Christians to refer to a heavenly judgment that began in 1844, marking the final phase of Christ's atoning work before His second coming.

In conclusion, the Day of Atonement was a critical observance in the Old Testament that provided a means for the annual cleansing of both the people and the sanctuary. The High Priest's duties and the rituals performed were rich in symbolic meaning, highlighting the seriousness of sin, the need for atonement, and the provision of God's grace. Prophetically, it pointed to the ultimate atonement achieved by Jesus Christ, our High Priest, who entered the heavenly sanctuary with His own blood to secure eternal redemption for all who believe. This understanding deepens our appreciation of Christ's redemptive work and its significance in the broader narrative of salvation history.

The death of Jesus Christ on the cross had profound implications for the sanctuary system, both earthly and heavenly. His sacrificial death marked a definitive turning point in the relationship between God and humanity, bringing fulfillment to the symbols and rituals of the Old Testament and inaugurating a new era of salvation through His heavenly ministry.

At the moment of Jesus' death, significant events occurred that symbolized the fulfillment of Old Testament prophecies and the transition to a new covenant. One of the most striking occurrences was the tearing of the temple veil. Matthew 27:51 records that at the moment Jesus breathed His last, "the curtain of the temple was torn in two, from top to bottom."

This veil, which separated the Holy Place from the Most Holy Place in the Temple, symbolized the barrier between God and humanity due to sin. Its tearing signified that through Christ's sacrifice, access to God was now open to all who believe. Hebrews 10:19-20 emphasizes this truth, stating that "we have confidence to enter the holy places by the blood of Jesus, by the new and living way that he opened for us through the curtain, that is, through his flesh."

The tearing of the temple veil also signified the end of the earthly sacrificial system. Hebrews 10:1-10 explains that the sacrifices offered under the Old Covenant were insufficient to cleanse the conscience and remove sin permanently. They served as a shadow of the ultimate sacrifice that Christ would offer. Jesus, as the Lamb of God, offered Himself once for all, fulfilling the requirements of the law and providing complete atonement for sin. Hebrews 10:10 states, "And by that will we have been sanctified through the offering of the body of Jesus Christ once for all."

The transition from the earthly sanctuary system to Christ's heavenly ministry is central to understanding the impact of His death. Hebrews chapters 8-10 elaborate on this transition, comparing the earthly sanctuary with its earthly high priests to Christ's ministry as the true High Priest in the heavenly sanctuary.

Hebrews 8:1-2 describes Christ as "a minister in the holy places, in the true tent that the Lord set up, not man." Unlike the earthly sanctuary, which required repeated sacrifices, Christ entered the heavenly sanctuary once for all, offering His own blood to secure eternal redemption for all who believe (Hebrews 9:11-12).

Christ's ministry in the heavenly sanctuary ensures the ongoing application of His atoning sacrifice to believers. Hebrews 7:25 affirms that "he is able to save to the uttermost those who draw near to God through him, since he always lives to make intercession for them." His intercession on our behalf ensures that the benefits of His sacrifice—forgiveness, cleansing, and reconciliation—are continuously applied, securing our standing before God and guaranteeing our eternal inheritance.

In conclusion, Jesus's death on the cross had a transformative impact on the sanctuary system. The tearing of the temple veil symbolized the removal of the barrier between God and humanity, granting access to God through Christ's sacrifice. His death marked the end of the earthly sacrificial system, fulfilled by His once-for-all sacrifice. This event inaugurated Christ's heavenly ministry as the true High Priest, where He continually intercedes for believers and applies the benefits of His atoning work. Understanding these truths deepens our appreciation for the completeness of Christ's redemption and underscores the centrality of His work in the plan of salvation.

Christ's ministry in the heavenly sanctuary is a central aspect of His ongoing work as our High Priest. Hebrews presents Jesus as the ultimate High Priest who entered the heavenly sanctuary, not with the blood of animals, but with His own blood, securing eternal redemption for all who believe (Hebrews 9:11-12). This ministry underscores His role as the mediator between God and humanity, ensuring the application of His atoning sacrifice and interceding on behalf of believers.

Hebrews 4:14-16 portrays Jesus as our sympathetic High Priest who understands our weaknesses because He has experienced human life yet without sin. He invites us to approach God's throne of grace with confidence, knowing that He intercedes for us. Romans 8:34 affirms this intercessory role, stating that Christ "is at the right hand of God, who indeed is interceding for us." His ongoing mediation ensures that our prayers are heard and our needs are presented before God.

The significance of Christ's ministry in the heavenly sanctuary for believers today cannot be overstated. It assures us of His constant presence and advocacy on our behalf. Through His intercession, Christ continues to apply the benefits of His sacrificial death—forgiveness, reconciliation, and eternal life—to all who come to God through Him. 1 Timothy 2:5 reinforces this truth, declaring that "there is one God, and there is one mediator between God and men, the man Christ Jesus."

Christ's ministry in the heavenly sanctuary provides believers with assurance and hope. It reminds us that our salvation is secure in Him and that He is actively involved in our lives, guiding us, comforting us, and empowering us through the Holy Spirit. His ministry assures us of God's faithfulness and His commitment to complete the work He has begun in us (Philippians 1:6).

Moreover, Christ's role as our High Priest in the heavenly sanctuary points to the fulfillment of God's redemptive plan. It emphasizes the continuity and completeness of His work, from His sacrificial death on the cross to His ongoing ministry in heaven. Revelation 1:18 declares Jesus as the One who "died, and behold I am alive forevermore, and I have the keys of Death and Hades." This victorious proclamation underscores His authority over sin and death, securing our ultimate victory and eternal inheritance.

In summary, Jesus's ministry in the heavenly sanctuary is foundational to the Christian faith. It highlights His role as our High Priest who offered Himself as the perfect sacrifice for sin and who continues to intercede for us before God's throne. His ministry ensures that believers have access to God's grace and mercy, empowering us to live boldly and confidently in His promises. Understanding and embracing Christ's ministry in the heavenly sanctuary deepens our faith, strengthens our relationship with God, and assures us of our eternal hope in Him.

The concept of the cleansing of the sanctuary, as described in Daniel 8:14, holds significant prophetic and theological implications within Christian eschatology. The verse states, "And he said to me, 'For 2,300 evenings and mornings. Then the sanctuary shall be restored to its rightful state.'" This prophecy points to a period of time after which the sanctuary would be cleansed or vindicated, signifying a divine judgment and restoration.

In Christian theology, particularly within Adventism and related denominations, this prophecy is understood to refer to a period of investigative judgment that began in 1844. According to this belief, Christ, as the heavenly High Priest, entered the Most Holy Place of the heavenly sanctuary to perform a final phase of judgment before His second coming. This investigative judgment is based on the records of human lives, determining the fitness of individuals for eternal life based on their response to God's grace and their acceptance of Christ's atoning sacrifice.

The cleansing of the heavenly sanctuary, therefore, involves a process of divine judgment and purification. It signifies the final removal of sin and its consequences from the universe, affirming the righteousness and justice of God's judgments. This concept is intricately tied to the idea of the final atonement, where the benefits of Christ's sacrifice are fully applied to God's people, ensuring their eternal redemption and vindicating God's character before the universe.

The investigative judgment is seen as a continuation and completion of Christ's ministry in the heavenly sanctuary. It reveals the thoroughness of God's grace and His commitment to justice and righteousness. Revelation 22:12 echoes this idea, with Jesus declaring, "Behold, I am coming soon, bringing my recompense with me, to repay each one for what he has done." This judgment is not a fearful event for believers in Christ but a confirmation of their faith and a demonstration of God's faithfulness in completing His redemptive work.

In conclusion, the cleansing of the sanctuary, based on Daniel 8:14 and interpreted through New Testament revelation, points to the culmination of God's plan of redemption. It involves a divine judgment process, beginning with Christ's ministry as our High Priest in the heavenly sanctuary and culminating in the investigative judgment and final atonement. This concept underscores the completeness of Christ's work, the assurance of salvation for believers, and the vindication of God's righteousness before all creation. Understanding the cleansing of the sanctuary deepens our appreciation for God's grace and His commitment to justice, inviting us to live in readiness and anticipation of Christ's return and the fulfillment of His kingdom.

The understanding of Christ's ministry in the heavenly sanctuary carries profound implications for believers in Christ. Hebrews 10:19-22 encourages us to approach God with confidence and assurance, "Therefore, brothers, since we have confidence to enter the holy places by the blood of Jesus, by the new and living way that he opened for us through the curtain, that is, through his flesh, and since we have a great priest over the house of God, let us draw near with a true heart in full assurance of faith, with our hearts sprinkled clean from an evil conscience and our bodies washed with pure water."

Believers are invited to live with the assurance of salvation, knowing that through Christ's atoning work, we have been cleansed from sin and reconciled to God. This assurance is not based on our own merits or efforts but on the finished work of Christ on the cross and His ongoing ministry as our High Priest in heaven. It empowers us to live with confidence, knowing that our standing before God is secure and that nothing can separate us from His love (Romans 8:38-39).

Moreover, the understanding of Christ's ministry in the heavenly sanctuary calls believers to live lives of faith, repentance, and holiness. Hebrews 12:14 urges us, "Strive for peace with everyone, and for the holiness without which no one will see the Lord." As we anticipate Christ's second coming and the final restoration of all things, we are called to live in readiness and expectation, actively pursuing righteousness and godliness in every aspect of our lives (2 Peter 3:11-12).

The anticipation of Christ's second coming serves as a beacon of hope and encouragement for believers. Revelation 22:20 captures this longing, with John recording the words of Jesus, "He who testifies to these things says, 'Surely I am coming soon.' Amen. Come, Lord Jesus!" This anticipation motivates us to live faithfully, sharing the message of salvation with others and preparing ourselves and the world for the glorious return of our Savior.

In conclusion, the implications of Christ's ministry in the heavenly sanctuary are transformative for believers. They offer assurance of salvation through Christ's atoning work, call us to a life of faith and holiness, and inspire anticipation of Christ's second coming and the ultimate restoration of all things. Understanding and embracing these truths deepen our relationship with God, strengthen our commitment to following Christ, and ignite within us a passion to live for His glory until He comes again in power and majesty.

The doctrine of Christ's ministry in the heavenly sanctuary is a foundational truth in Christian theology, rich with profound implications for believers. Throughout this chapter, we have explored the significance of Christ as our High Priest who entered the heavenly sanctuary with His own blood, securing eternal redemption for all who believe. His ministry ensures the ongoing application of His atoning sacrifice, providing assurance of salvation and access to God's grace and mercy.

The theological significance of Christ's ministry in the heavenly sanctuary underscores the completeness and sufficiency of His work on the cross. It fulfills the Old Testament types and shadows, revealing Christ as the ultimate fulfillment of the sacrificial system and the mediator between God and humanity. Hebrews portrays Him not only as the High Priest who offered Himself as the perfect sacrifice but also as the advocate who intercedes for us before the Father, ensuring our forgiveness and acceptance.

Practically, the doctrine of Christ's ministry in the heavenly sanctuary calls believers to live lives characterized by faith, repentance, and holiness. It invites us to approach God with confidence, knowing that through Christ, we have been reconciled and made righteous. This assurance empowers us to persevere in times of trial, to seek forgiveness when we stumble, and to pursue a life that honors God in thought, word, and deed.

As we anticipate Christ's second coming and the final restoration of all things, understanding and embracing the truth of Christ's ministry in the heavenly sanctuary deepens our faith and hope. It reminds us of God's faithfulness, His promise of eternal life, and His ultimate plan to redeem and restore His creation. Let us therefore strive to deepen our understanding of this crucial doctrine, allowing it to shape our beliefs, transform our lives, and inspire us to share the hope of Christ with a world in need of His grace.

May we continually draw near to God with full assurance of faith, living in readiness and expectation of Christ's glorious return, when we will dwell with Him forever in the fullness of His presence and love. Amen.

11. The Glorious Return of Christ

The Second Coming of Christ, often referred to as the Parousia, is a cornerstone of Christian eschatological belief, embodying the hope and fulfillment of God's redemptive plan. This doctrine asserts that Jesus Christ will return to earth in a visible, glorious, and triumphant manner to complete the salvation of His people, judge the living and the dead, and establish His eternal kingdom.

The Second Coming is deeply rooted in both Old and New Testament scriptures. Prophecies from the Old Testament, such as those found in Isaiah and Daniel, point to a future Messianic reign characterized by justice, peace, and righteousness. The New Testament provides a more detailed and explicit depiction of Christ's return, emphasizing its suddenness and the signs that will precede it. Passages from the Gospels, the Epistles, and the Book of Revelation collectively contribute to a comprehensive biblical portrait of this anticipated event.

The importance of the Second Coming in Christian theology cannot be overstated. It serves as the culmination of God's salvific work, marking the definitive end of the present age and the inauguration of the new creation. This event underscores the ultimate victory of Christ over sin, death, and evil, bringing about the final restoration of all things. For believers, the Second Coming is a source of profound hope and encouragement, affirming that their faith and perseverance will be rewarded.

Moreover, the doctrine of the Second Coming has practical implications for Christian living. It motivates believers to live in a state of readiness, characterized by holiness, godliness, and a commitment to the mission of evangelism. The anticipation of Christ's return fosters a sense of urgency in spreading the Gospel and making disciples, as Jesus Himself commanded.

In summary, the Second Coming of Christ is a vital aspect of Christian doctrine, encapsulating the promise of ultimate redemption and the establishment of God's eternal kingdom. Its significance permeates theological understanding and practical Christian living, offering both hope for the future and a call to faithful discipleship in the present.

The doctrine of the Second Coming of Christ is firmly rooted in the biblical narrative, with both the Old and New Testaments providing foundational support for this belief. Throughout scripture, prophecies and promises outline the return of the Messiah, culminating in a vivid portrayal of Christ's triumphant return.

In the Old Testament, prophecies concerning the Messiah's coming often blend both His first advent and His return. Isaiah 11:1-10 presents a vision of the Messianic kingdom, where a descendant of Jesse, David's father, will arise. This prophecy describes the Messiah endowed with the Spirit of the Lord, exhibiting wisdom, understanding, counsel, might, knowledge, and fear of the Lord. The passage paints a picture of a just and righteous ruler who will bring peace and harmony, not only among people but also in the natural world. This prophecy is a foretaste of the ultimate restoration and peace that will be fully realized at Christ's Second Coming.

Daniel 7:13-14 offers another profound Old Testament prophecy. Daniel sees "one like a son of man" coming with the clouds of heaven, a phrase Jesus later appropriates to describe Himself. This figure is presented before the Ancient of Days and is given dominion, glory, and a kingdom that will never be destroyed. This vision emphasizes the eternal and sovereign reign of the Messiah, which aligns with the

Christian understanding of Christ's Second Coming when He will establish His everlasting kingdom.

The New Testament provides a clearer and more detailed picture of the Second Coming. Jesus Himself speaks extensively about His return. In Matthew 24:29-31, He describes the cosmic disturbances that will precede His coming, with the sun darkened, the moon not giving its light, and the stars falling from the sky. Jesus then speaks of the Son of Man appearing in the clouds with power and great glory, sending His angels to gather His elect from the four winds. This passage highlights the visible and glorious nature of Christ's return, along with the gathering of believers.

Acts 1:9-11 recounts Jesus' ascension, where He is taken up into heaven before the eyes of His disciples. As they stand gazing into the sky, two angels appear and promise that Jesus will return in the same manner as they saw Him go into heaven. This promise underscores the literal and physical return of Christ, affirming the continuity between His ascension and His Second Coming.

Revelation 19:11-16 provides one of the most dramatic and vivid descriptions of the Second Coming. John sees heaven opened and a white horse, with Christ, called Faithful and True, riding it. He comes to judge and wage war in righteousness, with His eyes like a flame of fire and many crowns on His head. He is clothed in a robe dipped in blood, and His name is called The Word of God. The armies of heaven follow Him on white horses, and from His mouth comes a sharp sword with which to strike down the nations. He will rule them with a rod of iron and tread the winepress of the fury of the wrath of God Almighty. On His robe and thigh, He has a name written: King of kings and Lord of lords. This passage encapsulates the victorious and sovereign nature of Christ's return, His role as judge, and the final establishment of His kingdom.

Together, these Old and New Testament passages provide a robust biblical basis for the belief in the Second Coming of Christ. They emphasize the fulfillment of prophetic promises, the visible and glorious nature of His return, and the ultimate establishment of His righteous and eternal reign. For Christians, these scriptures are a source of hope and a call to faithful anticipation of their Lord's return.

The Bible outlines various signs that will precede the Second Coming of Christ, serving as indicators for believers to recognize the approaching fulfillment of this divine promise. These signs can be categorized into natural, societal, and cosmic phenomena, each contributing to the prophetic landscape that heralds Christ's return.

Natural signs are prominently mentioned in Jesus' discourse on the Mount of Olives, as recorded in the Gospels. Earthquakes are highlighted as a significant precursor to the end times. Throughout history, earthquakes have been a constant reminder of the earth's instability, but their frequency and intensity in the last days will be unprecedented, signaling the impending return of Christ.

Famines, another natural sign, have plagued humanity since ancient times, but in the eschatological context, they are seen as intensifying. The scarcity of food, coupled with economic instability and environmental challenges, will lead to widespread hunger and suffering, further emphasizing the urgency of the times.

Pestilences, or widespread diseases, are also foretold. The recent Covid-19 pandemic serves as a poignant example of how swiftly and devastatingly a pestilence can spread, affecting millions globally. Such pandemics are a stark reminder of the fragility of human life and the need for divine intervention and restoration.

Societal signs also play a critical role in identifying the approach of Christ's return. Moral decline is a pervasive issue, characterized by the erosion of ethical standards and the abandonment of traditional values. This decline is evident in various aspects of society, including increased corruption, dishonesty, and a general disregard for righteousness.

Increased wickedness is another societal sign, with the world witnessing rising levels of violence, crime, and lawlessness. This moral decay is not only a result of human sinfulness but also an indication of the spiritual battle intensifying as the end draws near.

The persecution of believers is a clear sign that the end times are approaching. Throughout history, Christians have faced persecution for their faith, but Jesus warned that in the last days, this persecution would escalate. Believers will be hated, betrayed, and even put to death because of their allegiance to Christ. This heightened persecution serves as a sobering reminder of the cost of discipleship and the need for steadfast faith.

Cosmic signs, described in vivid detail in the scriptures, also signal the imminent return of Christ. The darkening of the sun and moon is a dramatic event that will capture the world's attention. These celestial bodies, which have faithfully provided light for millennia, will suddenly cease to function as normal, plunging the earth into an eerie darkness that signifies divine intervention.

The falling stars, or meteor showers, will add to the celestial disturbances. These falling stars, combined with the darkened sun and moon, will create a sense of awe and terror, underscoring the supernatural nature of the times.

The heavens shaken, a phrase used to describe the cosmic upheaval, points to the profound changes that will occur in the universe. This shaking signifies a divine reordering of the heavens, preparing the way for Christ's return and the establishment of His kingdom.

Together, these natural, societal, and cosmic signs create a compelling narrative that points to the Second Coming of Christ. They serve as both warnings and reminders, urging believers to remain vigilant, faithful, and hopeful as they anticipate the fulfillment of God's redemptive plan. The convergence of these signs underscores the urgency of the times and the need for readiness, as the day of the Lord draws near.

The Second Coming of Christ is one of the most anticipated events in Christian eschatology, and its nature is described in vivid terms throughout the New Testament. This event will be characterized by its visible and glorious manifestation, its personal and bodily occurrence, and its sudden and unexpected arrival.

The visible and glorious nature of Christ's return is emphasized repeatedly in scripture. Unlike His first coming, which was marked by humility and obscurity, Christ's return will be an event witnessed by all. Jesus Himself declared that His coming would be like lightning that flashes and lights up the sky from one end to the other, unmistakable and visible to everyone (Luke 17:24). This visibility underscores the universal scope of His return, leaving no room for doubt or denial. The glory of Christ's return will be unparalleled, marked by the brilliance and majesty befitting the King of kings. He will come in the clouds of heaven with great power and glory, accompanied by His angels, and every eye will see Him (Matthew 24:30; Revelation 1:7). This manifestation will be a dramatic contrast to His first coming and will reveal His divine authority and splendor.

The personal and bodily nature of Christ's return is another crucial aspect. The same Jesus who ascended into heaven will come back in like manner (Acts 1:11). This assurance given by the angels at His ascension emphasizes the continuity between His ascension and His return. Christ's return will be a personal event, meaning He Himself will come back, not merely a spiritual presence or symbolic return. Furthermore, it will be a bodily return. Jesus, in His resurrected and glorified body, will come back to earth. This belief is rooted in the Christian understanding of the resurrection, where Jesus' physical body was raised and glorified, affirming that He remains fully God and fully human. His bodily return ensures that His coming will be tangible and real, not just a spiritual experience.

The sudden and unexpected nature of Christ's return adds to the urgency and anticipation surrounding this event. Jesus warned His followers to be always ready, for the Son of Man will come at an hour when they do not expect Him (Matthew 24:44). The metaphor of a thief in the night is often used to describe the unexpectedness of His return (1 Thessalonians 5:2; 2 Peter 3:10). This imagery highlights the need for constant vigilance and preparedness among believers. Despite the signs that will precede His return, the exact timing remains unknown, known only to the Father (Matthew 24:36). This unpredictability serves as a call to live in a state of readiness, maintaining faithfulness and devotion in anticipation of His arrival.

In summary, the nature of Christ's return is multifaceted and awe-inspiring. It will be a visible and glorious event, revealing His divine majesty to all the world. It will be personal and bodily, affirming the continuity of His identity and the reality of His coming. And it will be sudden and unexpected, urging believers to live with constant readiness and hope. This understanding of the Second Coming provides both a profound sense of anticipation and a practical call to faithful living as Christians await the return of their Lord and Savior.

The Second Coming of Christ is not only a momentous event in Christian eschatology but also serves several significant purposes within God's redemptive plan. These purposes include judging the living and the dead, gathering His elect, and establishing His eternal kingdom.

One of the primary purposes of Christ's return is to judge the living and the dead. Scripture clearly teaches that Jesus will return as the righteous judge who will execute judgment on all humanity. In Matthew 25:31-46, Jesus describes the final judgment, where He will separate the sheep from the goats, symbolizing the righteous and the wicked. The righteous will inherit eternal life, while the wicked will face eternal punishment.

This judgment will be based on how individuals responded to Jesus and His teachings, particularly in their treatment of others. The Apostle Paul also emphasizes this aspect in his letters, stating that we must all appear before the judgment seat of Christ to receive what is due for the things done in the body, whether good or bad (2

Corinthians 5:10). This judgment underscores the justice and holiness of God, ensuring that every action is accounted for and every individual receives their due recompense.

    Another key purpose of Christ's return is to gather His elect. Throughout the New Testament, there are numerous references to the gathering of believers at the end of the age. In Matthew 24:31, Jesus states that He will send His angels with a loud trumpet call to gather His elect from the four winds, from one end of the heavens to the other.

    This gathering signifies the ultimate fulfillment of God's promise to His people, bringing together all who have placed their faith in Christ. It is a moment of great hope and joy for believers, as they are brought into the presence of their Savior and united with fellow believers. This gathering also reflects the inclusivity and universality of the Gospel, as people from every nation, tribe, and language will be gathered to worship the Lamb (Revelation 7:9-10).

    The establishment of His eternal kingdom is another central purpose of Christ's return. The return of Christ marks the culmination of God's redemptive plan, where He will establish His kingdom in its fullness. This kingdom is characterized by justice, peace, and righteousness, and it will never end. In Revelation 21:1-4, John describes a vision of the new heaven and new earth, where God will dwell with His people, and there will be no more death, mourning, crying, or pain. The old order of things will have passed away, and everything will be made new. This kingdom is the ultimate realization of God's promises throughout scripture, where He will reign forever and ever. It is a kingdom where His will is perfectly done, and His glory is fully revealed. This establishment of the eternal kingdom signifies the final victory over sin, death, and evil, bringing about the complete restoration of creation.

    In summary, the purposes of Christ's return are profound and multifaceted. He will return to judge the living and the dead, ensuring that justice is served and righteousness prevails. He will gather His elect, fulfilling God's promise to bring His people into His presence. And He will establish His eternal kingdom, where His reign of peace and righteousness will be fully realized. These purposes highlight the comprehensive nature of God's redemptive plan and provide believers with a powerful hope and assurance as they anticipate the return of their Savior.

The Millennial Reign of Christ is a subject of considerable debate and interpretation within Christian theology. This period, often referred to as the Millennium, is based on Revelation 20:1-6, where it describes a thousand-year reign of Christ.

The interpretations of this reign fall into three primary categories: Premillennialism, Amillennialism, and Postmillennialism, each offering a distinct perspective on the nature and timing of the Millennium.

Premillennialism is the belief that Christ will return before the Millennium to establish His kingdom on earth and reign for a literal thousand years. This interpretation is divided into two main subgroups: historic premillennialism and dispensational premillennialism. Historic premillennialists see the Millennium as the culmination of history where Christ's reign will visibly manifest His justice and peace.

Dispensational premillennialists, on the other hand, often include a pre-tribulation rapture, where believers are taken up before a period of great tribulation, followed by Christ's return and the establishment of His thousand-year reign. The biblical basis for premillennialism primarily stems from a literal reading of Revelation 20:1-6, along with Old Testament prophecies and New Testament passages that describe a future earthly kingdom where Christ reigns with His saints.

Amillennialism interprets the Millennium not as a literal thousand-year period but as a symbolic representation of the current church age, where Christ reigns spiritually in the hearts of believers and through the church. Amillennialists argue that the binding of Satan described in Revelation 20:1-3 occurred at Christ's first coming, and the "thousand years" is symbolic of a long, indefinite period. They view the resurrection mentioned in Revelation 20:4-6 as a spiritual resurrection, referring to the new birth and regeneration of believers. The biblical basis for amillennialism includes passages that emphasize the already-not-yet aspect of God's kingdom, where Christ's reign is already inaugurated but not yet fully consummated (e.g., Luke 17:20-21; Colossians 1:13). The theological implications of amillennialism stress the present reality of Christ's kingship and the church's role in advancing His kingdom through spiritual means.

Postmillennialism holds that Christ will return after the Millennium, which is understood as a golden age of Christian influence and societal transformation. According to this view, the gospel will progressively triumph over evil, leading to a period of peace and righteousness before Christ's return.

Postmillennialists see the Millennium as either a literal thousand years or a symbolic long period during which the world is increasingly Christianized. The biblical basis for postmillennialism includes passages that speak of the growth and ultimate victory of God's kingdom (e.g., Matthew 13:31-33; Isaiah 2:2-4). The theological implications of postmillennialism emphasize the power of the gospel to transform society and the optimistic view that Christ's reign will be realized through the church's mission and influence.

Each of these interpretations carries significant theological implications. Premillennialism highlights the future hope of Christ's physical reign on earth and the ultimate fulfillment of God's promises to Israel and the church. It encourages believers to anticipate Christ's return with a sense of urgency and preparedness.

Amillennialism underscores the current spiritual reign of Christ and the ongoing battle against spiritual forces, encouraging believers to live out their faith actively and advance God's kingdom in the present age. Postmillennialism inspires a vision of cultural and societal transformation through the power of the gospel, motivating believers to engage in mission and social justice with the confidence that Christ's kingdom will ultimately prevail.

In summary, the Millennial Reign of Christ is interpreted differently across Christian traditions, with premillennialism, amillennialism, and postmillennialism offering distinct perspectives on its nature and timing. The biblical basis for each interpretation varies, and the theological implications shape how believers understand the unfolding of God's redemptive plan and their role in it. Despite these differences, all views converge on the hope and assurance that Christ will ultimately reign in victory, bringing about the final consummation of His kingdom.

The Seventh-day Adventist (SDA) interpretation of the Millennial Reign of Christ aligns closely with a form of premillennialism, but it carries distinct nuances that reflect the denomination's emphasis on eschatology and the great controversy theme between Christ and Satan. According to SDA theology, the Millennium is a literal thousand-year period that follows the Second Coming of Christ and precedes the final destruction of sin and the recreation of the new earth.

Seventh-day Adventists believe that at Christ's Second Coming, the righteous dead will be resurrected and, along with the living righteous, will be taken to heaven to reign with Christ for a thousand years. This event is referred to as the first resurrection. During this time, the earth will be desolate, a "bottomless pit" where Satan and his angels are bound with no one to tempt or deceive. This binding of Satan is not a physical restraint but rather a situational one, as the wicked are all dead, and there are no human beings left on earth for him to influence.

The Millennium serves several critical purposes in SDA theology. One significant aspect is the judgment. The saints, during this thousand-year period, will participate in a process of judgment, examining the records of the wicked to understand the justice and fairness of God's decisions. This is often referred to as the "millennial judgment" and is seen as a time for the righteous to be fully assured of God's righteous judgments before the final execution of judgment at the end of the Millennium.

At the close of the Millennium, Christ, along with the redeemed and the Holy City, the New Jerusalem, will descend from heaven to earth. This event triggers the second resurrection, also known as the resurrection of the wicked. Satan is then released from his "prison" as he now has people to deceive once again. He will rally the resurrected wicked for a final assault on the New Jerusalem. However, this last rebellion is quickly quashed, as fire comes down from God out of heaven and consumes them. This event, known as the "second death," results in the complete and eternal destruction of the wicked and the eradication of sin.

Following this final judgment and the purification of the earth by fire, God will create a new heaven and a new earth. The redeemed will then inhabit this new creation, where there will be no more death, sorrow, crying, or pain. The former things will have passed away, and God will dwell with His people in perfect harmony forever.

The SDA interpretation of the Millennium emphasizes the ultimate vindication of God's character. Through the processes of the first and second resurrections, the binding and loosing of Satan, and the millennial judgment, the great controversy between Christ and Satan is brought to a close. God's justice, mercy, and love are demonstrated to the entire universe, and His righteous rule is affirmed.

In summary, the Seventh-day Adventist view of the Millennial Reign of Christ involves a literal thousand-year period following the Second Coming, during which the righteous reign with Christ in heaven, the wicked are dead, and Satan is bound on a desolate earth. This period includes a judgment phase where the righteous review the records of the wicked, culminating in the final destruction of sin and the creation of a new heaven and new earth. This interpretation highlights the themes of divine justice, the resolution of the great controversy, and the ultimate restoration of harmony in God's creation.

The culmination of God's redemptive plan is the creation of the New Heaven and New Earth, a theme woven throughout scripture and reaching its climax in the final chapters of Revelation. This profound transformation represents the complete restoration of creation, the eternal dwelling of humanity with God, and the ultimate fulfillment of God's divine purpose.

The restoration of creation is a central aspect of the New Heaven and New Earth. In the beginning, God created a perfect world, but sin marred this perfection, bringing death, decay, and suffering into the world.

Throughout history, the effects of sin have been evident in the brokenness of creation. However, the promise of a New Heaven and New Earth signifies God's commitment to restore all things to their original, untainted state. In Revelation 21:1, John describes seeing a new heaven and a new earth, for the first heaven and the first earth had passed away. This renewal is not just a return to the original creation but an elevation to an even more glorious state.

It is a place where there is no more death, mourning, crying, or pain, for the old order of things has passed away (Revelation 21:4). The restoration of creation encompasses both the physical and the spiritual, with nature itself liberated from its bondage to decay and brought into the glorious freedom of the children of God (Romans 8:21).

The eternal dwelling with God is another defining feature of the New Heaven and New Earth. The separation caused by sin is finally and completely overcome, and God's people will dwell in His presence forever. Revelation 21:3 captures this profound reality: "And I heard a loud voice from the throne saying, 'Look! God's dwelling place is now among the people, and he will dwell with them. They will be his people, and God himself will be with them and be their God.'"

This promise fulfills the deepest longings of the human heart for communion with the Creator. In this eternal dwelling, there will be no temple, for the Lord God Almighty and the Lamb are its temple (Revelation 21:22). The intimate relationship between God and humanity, once disrupted by sin, will be perfectly restored. The redeemed will see God face to face and will serve Him in eternal joy and fellowship (Revelation 22:3-4). The eternal presence of God will illuminate the New Jerusalem, eliminating the need for any other source of light (Revelation 21:23). This eternal dwelling signifies a relationship of unparalleled closeness, love, and unity between God and His people.

The New Heaven and New Earth also represent the ultimate fulfillment of God's plan. From the beginning, God's intention was to dwell with His creation in a perfect and harmonious relationship. The entirety of redemptive history—starting from the fall of humanity, through the covenants with Israel, the coming of Jesus Christ, His death and resurrection, and the establishment of the church—points towards this final fulfillment. The New Heaven and New Earth bring God's redemptive work to its glorious conclusion. It is a realization of the divine promise that God's dwelling place will be with humanity, and He will be their God.

This fulfillment is not merely a return to Eden but an even greater reality where God's plan for creation reaches its highest expression. The ultimate defeat of sin and death, the eradication of all suffering, and the renewal of all things reflect the perfect wisdom, justice, and love of God. In this eternal state, the redeemed will reign with Christ forever, experiencing the fullness of life as God originally intended (Revelation 22:5). This ultimate fulfillment is the manifestation of God's kingdom in its complete form, where His will is done perfectly and His glory is fully revealed.

In summary, the New Heaven and New Earth encompass the restoration of creation to a state of perfect harmony, the eternal dwelling of humanity with God in intimate fellowship, and the ultimate fulfillment of God's redemptive plan. This vision offers profound hope and assurance to believers, providing a glimpse of the eternal joy and peace that await in God's perfect kingdom.

As Christians anticipate the Second Coming of Christ, the call to prepare becomes an essential part of their faith journey. This preparation encompasses living in holiness and godliness, watching and waiting for Christ's return, and engaging in evangelism and mission. Each of these aspects reflects a faithful response to the hope and promise of Christ's imminent return.

Living in holiness and godliness is a foundational aspect of preparing for the Second Coming. The Apostle Peter, in his second epistle, emphasizes this call to holiness: "Since everything will be destroyed in this way, what kind of people ought you to be? You ought to live holy and godly lives as you look forward to the day of God and speed its coming" (2 Peter 3:11-12).

Holiness involves setting oneself apart for God, striving to reflect His character in every aspect of life. This means pursuing righteousness, turning away from sin, and embodying the fruits of the Spirit—love, joy, peace, patience, kindness, goodness, faithfulness, gentleness, and self-control (Galatians 5:22-23). Living in godliness involves a deep reverence for God, manifested in obedience to His will and a life committed to His service. It is an ongoing process of sanctification, where believers grow in their relationship with God and become more like Christ. This pursuit of holiness and godliness serves as a testimony to the transformative power of the Gospel and prepares believers for the return of their Lord.

Watching and waiting are also crucial elements of preparation. Jesus frequently taught His disciples about the importance of being watchful and ready for His return. In Matthew 24:42, He admonishes, "Therefore keep watch, because you do not know on what day your Lord will come." This watchfulness involves a state of spiritual alertness, where believers remain attentive to the signs of the times and the promptings of the Holy Spirit. It is a call to live with a sense of expectancy, knowing that Christ's return could happen at any moment.

Waiting, in this context, is not passive but active. It involves persevering in faith, maintaining hope, and continuing in prayer. The parable of the ten virgins (Matthew 25:1-13) illustrates the necessity of being prepared, highlighting the wise virgins who were ready with their lamps and oil when the bridegroom arrived. Believers are called to be like the wise virgins, staying prepared and vigilant, so they are ready to welcome Christ when He comes.

Evangelism and mission are integral to preparing for the Second Coming, as they align with the Great Commission given by Jesus to His disciples. Before ascending to heaven, Jesus instructed His followers, "Go and make disciples of all nations, baptizing them in the name of the Father and of the Son and of the Holy Spirit, and teaching them to obey everything I have commanded you" (Matthew 28:19-20).

This mandate underscores the urgency and importance of sharing the Gospel with others, inviting them into a saving relationship with Christ. Evangelism involves proclaiming the good news of Jesus Christ—His life, death, resurrection, and imminent return. It is about bearing witness to the transformative power of His grace and love. Mission, on the other hand, encompasses the broader work of advancing God's kingdom through acts of service, justice, and compassion. It involves addressing the physical, emotional, and spiritual needs of others, reflecting Christ's love in tangible ways. Engaging in evangelism and mission not only fulfills Christ's command but also helps prepare the world for His return, as more people come to know and follow Him.

In summary, preparing for the Second Coming of Christ involves living in holiness and godliness, watching and waiting with expectancy, and engaging in evangelism and mission. These aspects reflect a faithful and active response to the promise of Christ's return, encouraging believers to live lives that honor God and advance His kingdom. By doing so, they not only prepare themselves but also help others to be ready for the glorious day when Christ returns to establish His eternal reign.

The hope and assurance of Christ's return stand as a beacon of promise and fulfillment for believers throughout history. From the earliest writings of the prophets to the teachings of Jesus Himself and the apostolic letters, the Second Coming of Christ has been a central theme of Christian faith. This blessed hope is not merely a distant future event but a reality that shapes the present lives of believers.

The promise of Christ's return provides unwavering hope in the midst of uncertainty and challenges. It assures believers that God's redemptive plan will reach its ultimate culmination, bringing justice, restoration, and eternal life to all who have placed their trust in Him. This hope inspires confidence in God's faithfulness and encourages perseverance in the face of trials. As the Apostle Paul wrote, "We wait for the blessed hope—the appearing of the glory of our great God and Savior, Jesus Christ" (Titus 2:13).

For believers, the prospect of Christ's return is a source of encouragement and motivation. It prompts them to live faithfully, knowing that their labor in the Lord is not in vain (1 Corinthians 15:58). It spurs them to love one another fervently, to pursue righteousness, and to walk in obedience to God's Word. The imminent return of Christ compels believers to prioritize eternal values over temporal pursuits, to seek first the kingdom of God and His righteousness (Matthew 6:33).

In conclusion, let us heed the final exhortation of Scripture to remain faithful and watchful as we await the glorious return of our Lord. Jesus Himself said, "Behold, I am coming soon! My reward is with me, and I will give to each person according to what they have done" (Revelation 22:12). Therefore, let us fix our eyes on Jesus, the author and perfecter of our faith (Hebrews 12:2), and live each day in readiness and anticipation of His coming. May His grace sustain us, His Spirit guide us, and His love empower us until that day when we shall see Him face to face and dwell with Him forever in the new heavens and new earth. Amen.

12. Life Beyond Death

Death is a subject that touches every human life, and for many, it raises profound questions about the meaning of existence and what, if anything, lies beyond. In this chapter, we aim to explore the Christian understanding of death, the state of the dead, and the hope of resurrection. By delving into biblical teachings and theological reflections, we seek to provide clarity and comfort on these deeply significant topics.

The purpose of this chapter is to present a comprehensive examination of the Christian perspective on death and what follows. We will look into the nature of death, considering it both as a universal human experience and as a consequence of sin, as described in the Bible. From there, we will explore what Scripture and Christian doctrine say about the state of the dead, addressing questions about consciousness after death, the concept of the soul, and what happens between death and the final resurrection.

The state of the dead is a particularly complex topic with varied interpretations. We will discuss the Old Testament views on the afterlife, which often centered around Sheol, and compare these with New Testament teachings, where Jesus and Paul introduce ideas like "sleep" to describe death. By examining these perspectives, we aim to understand how they have shaped Christian beliefs over the centuries.

The concept of resurrection is central to Christian hope. This chapter will cover the Old Testament prophecies that hinted at resurrection, such as those found in Daniel and Ezekiel, and then move to the New Testament, focusing on the resurrection of Jesus Christ as the cornerstone of Christian faith. We will consider the evidence and significance of Christ's resurrection, as well as the promise of a general resurrection at the end of time. This promise includes the transformation of believers and the ultimate defeat of death.

By the end of this chapter, readers will have a thorough understanding of the Christian doctrines concerning death, the intermediate state, and resurrection. These beliefs provide hope and assurance, influencing how Christians live and face the reality of mortality. This exploration will not only deepen theological knowledge but also offer practical insights for living a life grounded in the promise of eternal life.

Death, from a Christian perspective, is a multifaceted phenomenon that holds both profound theological significance and deep emotional resonance. Theologically, death is not merely an end but a part of the broader narrative of creation, fall, redemption, and restoration. It is a subject deeply embedded in the fabric of Christian doctrine and the biblical story.

In the Bible, death is defined and described in various ways, often reflecting its complexity and gravity. In the Old Testament, death is frequently portrayed as a return to the dust from which humanity was formed, a poignant reminder of our mortal nature (Genesis 3:19). The Psalms and prophetic writings speak of death as a descent into Sheol, a shadowy place where the dead reside (Psalm 6:5, Isaiah 14:9). In the New Testament, death is often referred to metaphorically as "sleep," particularly in the teachings of Jesus and Paul, indicating a temporary state preceding resurrection (John 11:11, 1 Thessalonians 4:13-14).

The significance of death in the human experience cannot be overstated. It is a universal reality that evokes a wide range of emotions, from fear and sorrow to contemplation and hope. For Christians, death is seen through the lens of faith, where it is not merely an end but a transition to a different form of existence. It is an event that, while often painful, is also a reminder of the temporal nature of life and the eternal promise of God.

Death is intrinsically linked to the concept of sin in Christian theology. According to the Bible, death entered the world as a direct consequence of human disobedience. The Genesis account of the Fall describes how Adam and Eve's choice to eat from the forbidden tree brought sin and death into God's perfect creation (Genesis 3). This narrative underscores the belief that death is not part of God's original design for humanity but a result of the rupture in the relationship between God and humankind.

The Apostle Paul succinctly captures this connection in his epistle to the Romans: "For the wages of sin is death, but the gift of God is eternal life in Christ Jesus our Lord" (Romans 6:23). This verse highlights the dual reality of human existence: while sin leads to death, God's grace offers the promise of eternal life. Death, therefore, is not the final word; it is a consequence of sin that has been overcome through the redemptive work of Jesus Christ.

In Christian thought, the understanding of death as both a consequence of sin and a gateway to eternal life provides a framework for addressing its mystery and pain. It allows believers to confront death with a sense of hope, rooted in the belief that Jesus' death and resurrection have conquered the power of death. This hope is central to the Christian faith, offering comfort in the face of loss and a promise of future restoration and reunion with God.

Through this lens, death becomes a profound theological and existential reality that shapes the Christian narrative. It reminds believers of their dependence on God's grace and the ultimate victory of life over death through Jesus Christ. In this context, death is not an end but a critical chapter in the divine story of salvation and eternal life.

The question of what happens after death has intrigued humanity for millennia, and the Bible provides a multifaceted view of the state of the dead. This section will explore the perspectives offered by both the

Old and New Testaments, as well as various doctrinal interpretations within Christianity.

In the Old Testament, the afterlife is often depicted in terms of Sheol, a place where the dead reside. Sheol is described as a shadowy, indistinct realm beneath the earth where both the righteous and the wicked go after death (Psalm 6:5, Ecclesiastes 9:10). It is portrayed as a place of stillness and darkness, lacking the vibrancy of earthly life. The grave, or the pit, is similarly seen as a destination where the dead are cut off from the living and from God's active presence (Isaiah 38:18, Job 17:13-16). These descriptions emphasize the finality and mystery surrounding death.

Prophetic insights and the Psalms offer glimpses of hope beyond Sheol. For instance, Psalm 16:10 expresses confidence that God will not abandon the faithful to Sheol, hinting at a future redemption. Isaiah and Ezekiel contain visions that suggest resurrection and restoration, such as the valley of dry bones coming to life (Ezekiel 37) and the promise of God swallowing up death forever (Isaiah 25:8). These passages sow seeds of a future hope that will be more fully developed in the New Testament.

The New Testament brings a significant shift in understanding the state of the dead, primarily through the teachings of Jesus and the apostles. Jesus frequently referred to death as sleep, implying a temporary condition from which one will awaken (John 11:11-14). He taught about a future resurrection and eternal life, offering assurances that those who believe in Him will have life beyond physical death (John 5:24-29, John 11:25-26).

Paul's letters further elaborate on this concept. He often used the metaphor of sleep to describe the state of believers who have died, emphasizing the hope of resurrection (1 Thessalonians 4:13-18, 1 Corinthians 15:20). Paul taught that at the return of Christ, the dead in Christ will rise first, and then the living will be transformed, highlighting the continuity and renewal of life beyond death.

Doctrinal interpretations within Christianity vary regarding the state of the dead. One major debate centers on the immortality of the soul versus conditional immortality. The traditional view holds that the soul is inherently immortal and continues to exist consciously after death, either in heaven or hell. This view is supported by passages that speak of the eternal nature of the soul (Matthew 25:46).

Conditional immortality, on the other hand, argues that immortality is a gift granted only to the righteous. According to this view, the wicked face annihilation rather than eternal torment, aligning with scriptures that speak of the final destruction of the wicked (Matthew 10:28, Revelation 20:14-15).

The concept of soul sleep posits that the dead are in a state of unconsciousness until the resurrection. Proponents of this view interpret biblical references to sleep as indicative of a lack of awareness in death (Ecclesiastes 9:5-6, 1 Thessalonians 4:13-15). This doctrine suggests that the dead are not aware of the passage of time until they are awakened at the resurrection.

Another related concept is the intermediate state, the period between death and the final resurrection. Some Christian traditions, particularly Catholicism, teach the existence of purgatory, where souls undergo purification before entering heaven. Others, especially in Protestant traditions, reject this idea, instead believing that the dead immediately enter either heaven or hell upon death, pending the final resurrection and judgment.

In summary, the state of the dead in Christian theology encompasses a range of beliefs informed by both Old and New Testament teachings. While the Old Testament provides a more shadowy view of Sheol and the grave, the New Testament brings clarity and hope through the teachings of Jesus and the apostles on resurrection and eternal life. The various doctrinal interpretations further enrich the understanding of what happens after death, offering different perspectives on the nature of the soul and the intermediate state. Ultimately, these beliefs converge on the hope of resurrection and the promise of eternal life with God.

The doctrine of resurrection lies at the heart of Christian hope, promising new life beyond death. This belief is rooted in the Old Testament, brought to fulfillment in the resurrection of Jesus Christ, and culminates in the promise of a general resurrection at the end of time.

In the Old Testament, the idea of resurrection is not fully developed but is hinted at through various prophetic visions and declarations. One of the clearest references is found in Daniel 12:2, which speaks of a future time when "many of those who sleep in the dust of the earth shall awake, some to everlasting life, and some to shame and everlasting contempt." This prophecy introduces the notion of a bodily resurrection, where the dead are raised to face either reward or judgment.

Ezekiel's vision of the dry bones further enriches the Old Testament foundation for resurrection. In Ezekiel 37, the prophet sees a valley filled with dry bones that come to life, symbolizing the restoration of Israel. This vision not only points to the hope of national renewal but also resonates with the theme of individual resurrection, as the breath of God brings the dead back to life. These prophetic glimpses lay the groundwork for the more explicit teachings on resurrection found in the New Testament.

The resurrection of Jesus Christ stands as the cornerstone of Christian faith and theology. Historically, it is the event that transformed a group of frightened disciples into bold proclaimers of the gospel. Theologically, it signifies the defeat of death and the inauguration of a new creation. Jesus' resurrection is presented in the Gospels with compelling detail and numerous eyewitness accounts. Mary Magdalene and other women were the first to witness the empty tomb, followed by appearances to the apostles and over five hundred other followers (Matthew 28:1-10, 1 Corinthians 15:3-8). These accounts emphasize the physical nature of Jesus' resurrection, where He could be touched and seen, yet also possessed a glorified body.

The resurrection of Jesus is not an isolated event but the firstfruits of a larger harvest. The New Testament teaches that just as Christ was raised from the dead, so too will all people experience resurrection. In 1 Corinthians 15, Paul provides a comprehensive discussion on the nature and timing of the resurrection. He explains that at Christ's return, the dead will be raised imperishable, and those who are alive will be transformed. This transformation involves the corruptible putting on incorruption and the mortal putting on immortality, highlighting a radical renewal of the human body.

Paul further elaborates on this transformation in Philippians 3:20-21, where he speaks of the believer's citizenship in heaven and the awaited Savior, Jesus Christ, who "will transform our lowly body to be like his glorious body, by the power that enables him even to subject all things to himself." This promise of a glorified body assures believers that resurrection is not merely a return to earthly life but an entry into a new, perfected existence.

The general resurrection also encompasses the righteous and the wicked. Jesus taught that all who are in their graves will hear His voice and come out—those who have done good to the resurrection of life, and those who have done evil to the resurrection of judgment (John 5:28-29). This dual outcome underscores the moral and eschatological dimensions of resurrection, where final judgment and eternal destinies are determined.

In conclusion, the doctrine of resurrection in Christian theology provides profound hope and assurance. It is deeply rooted in Old Testament prophecies and visions, brought to fruition in the resurrection of Jesus Christ, and promises a future resurrection for all humanity. This hope of new life transforms the way believers understand death and motivates a life of faithfulness, knowing that death is not the end but a transition to a glorious, eternal future with God.

The doctrine of resurrection carries significant eschatological implications, shaping Christian understanding of the end times, the Second Coming of Christ, and the final judgment. It also offers the promise of eternal life, which influences how believers live with hope and assurance in their daily lives.

The resurrection is intimately connected with the broader eschatological framework of the end times. According to Christian teaching, the resurrection of the dead will occur at the end of the age, coinciding with the return of Jesus Christ. This Second Coming is depicted as a glorious and transformative event, where Christ will descend from heaven with a commanding shout, accompanied by the voice of the archangel and the trumpet call of God. At this moment, the dead in Christ will rise first, followed by the transformation of those who are still alive (1 Thessalonians 4:16-17). This event marks the consummation of God's redemptive plan, where the faithful are gathered to be with the Lord forever.

The Second Coming also heralds the final judgment, a central theme in Christian eschatology. At this time, all people, both living and dead, will stand before the judgment seat of Christ. The Book of Revelation provides a vivid depiction of this event, describing the opening of books that record the deeds of every individual (Revelation 20:11-15). Those whose names are written in the Book of Life will enter eternal life, while those not found in the book will face eternal separation from God. This judgment underscores the moral accountability of every person and the ultimate justice of God.

The promise of eternal life is a cornerstone of Christian hope, offering believers a future that transcends the trials and tribulations of the present world. Eternal life is not merely an unending existence but a quality of life characterized by perfect communion with God. Jesus described this life as knowing God and Jesus Christ, whom He has sent (John 17:3). This intimate relationship with God is the essence of eternal life, promising fulfillment, joy, and peace that surpasses all understanding.

Living with this hope and assurance profoundly impacts Christian living. The promise of resurrection and eternal life gives believers the strength to endure suffering and hardship, knowing that their present struggles are temporary and pale in comparison to the glory that awaits them (Romans 8:18). This eschatological perspective encourages a life of faithfulness, perseverance, and holiness, as Christians seek to align their lives with the values of God's coming kingdom.

Practically, this hope manifests in various ways. It motivates believers to engage in acts of love, service, and compassion, reflecting the character of Christ in their interactions with others. The assurance of eternal life also fosters a sense of peace and contentment, freeing believers from the fear of death and the anxieties of this world. Moreover, it instills a sense of purpose and mission, as Christians are called to witness to the reality of God's kingdom and invite others into the hope they have received.

In conclusion, the eschatological implications of the doctrine of resurrection are profound and far-reaching. They shape the Christian understanding of the end times, the Second Coming of Christ, and the final judgment, providing a framework for comprehending the ultimate destiny of humanity. The promise of eternal life offers a source of hope and assurance, empowering believers to live with purpose, faithfulness, and joy. This eschatological hope transforms the way Christians view their present circumstances, infusing their lives with a sense of divine purpose and the confident expectation of a glorious future with God.

The doctrine of death, the state of the dead, and resurrection has not been without its controversies and debates within Christianity. Varied interpretations of these concepts have led to differing theological perspectives, each seeking to understand the nature of the soul, the afterlife, and the events that follow death.

Within the broad spectrum of Christian thought, traditional views have often emphasized the immortality of the soul and the immediate transition to either heaven or hell upon death. This perspective is deeply rooted in centuries of theological development and scriptural interpretation. According to this view, the soul continues to exist consciously after death, awaiting the final resurrection and judgment. Heaven is seen as the eternal dwelling place for the righteous, while hell is the eternal punishment for the wicked. This dualistic view has shaped much of Christian teaching and liturgy, offering a clear and immediate dichotomy between the saved and the lost.

However, modern perspectives have introduced alternative interpretations that challenge traditional views. Some contemporary theologians advocate for conditional immortality, which posits that only the righteous receive eternal life as a gift from God, while the wicked face annihilation. This view emphasizes the conditional nature of immortality, aligning with scriptural references to the destruction of the wicked (Matthew 10:28, Revelation 20:14-15). Proponents argue that this perspective is more consistent with the character of a just and loving God.

Another modern interpretation is the concept of soul sleep, which suggests that the dead enter a state of unconsciousness until the resurrection. This view is based on biblical passages that describe death as sleep, implying a lack of awareness until the final awakening (Ecclesiastes 9:5-6, 1 Thessalonians 4:13-15). Advocates of soul sleep argue that this interpretation avoids the philosophical difficulties associated with disembodied existence and provides a more coherent understanding of the intermediate state.

The nature of the soul and the afterlife has been a focal point of theological debates throughout Christian history. Questions about whether the soul is inherently immortal or conditionally so have prompted extensive discussion among theologians. Additionally, the nature of hell—whether it is a place of eternal conscious torment, a temporary state leading to annihilation, or a metaphorical expression of separation from God—remains a contentious issue. These debates reflect the diversity of thought within Christianity and the complexity of interpreting scriptural teachings on these profound topics.

Addressing common questions and misconceptions about what happens immediately after death is crucial for providing clarity and comfort to believers. One of the most frequently asked questions is whether the soul goes directly to heaven or hell upon death or remains in an unconscious state until the resurrection. Traditional views typically support the idea of an immediate transition to the afterlife, based on passages like the parable of the rich man and Lazarus (Luke 16:19-31) and Jesus' promise to the thief on the cross (Luke 23:43). However, proponents of soul sleep interpret these passages differently, suggesting that they are metaphorical or specific to particular contexts rather than universal statements about the afterlife.

Another common question is how Christians should respond to death and loss. The Christian response to death is deeply rooted in the hope of resurrection and eternal life. While death is a source of grief and sorrow, it is also seen as a passage to a promised future with God. Christians are encouraged to mourn with hope, knowing that death does not have the final word (1 Thessalonians 4:13). The assurance of resurrection and the promise of eternal life provide comfort and strength in the face of loss. Additionally, the Christian community plays a vital role in supporting those who grieve, offering compassion, prayer, and practical assistance.

In conclusion, the doctrine of death, the state of the dead, and resurrection encompasses a range of interpretations and debates within Christianity. Traditional views emphasize the immediate transition to heaven or hell, while modern perspectives such as conditional immortality and soul sleep offer alternative understandings.

Theological debates on the nature of the soul and the afterlife continue to shape Christian thought, reflecting the diversity and complexity of these topics. Addressing common questions and misconceptions helps provide clarity and comfort to believers, grounding them in the hope of resurrection and the assurance of eternal life.

In this chapter, we have explored the profound and multifaceted Christian doctrines surrounding death, the state of the dead, and resurrection. These concepts, deeply rooted in both the Old and New Testaments, offer believers a framework for understanding mortality and the promise of new life.

We began by examining the theological perspectives on death, recognizing it as both a universal human experience and a consequence of sin. The Genesis account of the Fall and Paul's declaration in Romans 6:23 illustrate how death entered the world through disobedience but is ultimately overcome by the gift of eternal life in Christ Jesus.

The state of the dead was then considered from both Old Testament and New Testament viewpoints. The Old Testament's depiction of Sheol as a place of shadowy existence and the prophetic glimpses of future resurrection laid the groundwork for the New Testament's more developed teachings. Jesus' and Paul's references to death as sleep, along with the promise of resurrection, provide believers with a hopeful perspective on what lies beyond death.

The resurrection of Jesus Christ was highlighted as the cornerstone of Christian faith, signifying victory over death and offering a foretaste of the general resurrection to come. The historical and theological significance of Jesus' resurrection, supported by eyewitness accounts, reinforces the promise of new life for all believers. Paul's teachings in 1 Corinthians 15 and Philippians 3 further elucidate the nature of this resurrection and the transformation of the body, providing a vivid picture of the hope that awaits.

We also delved into the eschatological implications of resurrection, including its role in the end times, the Second Coming of Christ, and the final judgment. These events underscore the ultimate justice of God and the fulfillment of His redemptive plan, culminating in the promise of eternal life. This hope empowers believers to live with assurance and purpose, influencing their daily lives and interactions with others.

The chapter addressed the varied interpretations and debates within Christianity regarding the nature of the soul and the afterlife. By exploring traditional views, modern perspectives, and theological debates, we gained a deeper understanding of the complexities and nuances surrounding these doctrines. Addressing common questions and misconceptions about what happens after death and how Christians should respond to loss provided clarity and comfort.

In reflecting on these key points, it is essential to encourage believers to hold fast to the hope of resurrection and eternal life. Death, while a source of sorrow, is not the end but a transition to a glorious future with God. The promise of resurrection offers a profound source of comfort and strength, enabling believers to face mortality with confidence and peace. Final reflections on death, the state of the dead, and resurrection remind us of the centrality of these doctrines to the Christian faith. They shape our understanding of life, death, and what lies beyond, grounding us in the assurance that through Christ, death has been defeated and eternal life secured. As we live out our faith, may we do so with the hope and assurance that we are part of God's redemptive story, destined for a future where death is no more and life eternal with God awaits.

13. Hope for a Renewed Creation

The purpose of this chapter is to explore the theological concept of the Millennium and its profound significance within Christian eschatology. The Millennium refers to a thousand-year period often associated with Christ's reign on earth, marking a time of peace, justice, and spiritual renewal. This chapter aims to examine the biblical foundations, various interpretations, and eschatological implications of the Millennium. By delving into these key concepts, we seek to illuminate how beliefs about the Millennium shape Christian hope for a future characterized by the complete triumph over sin and the establishment of God's kingdom in its fullness.

The concept of the Millennium finds its roots in both Old and New Testament scriptures, which provide foundational teachings and prophetic glimpses of a future age characterized by the reign of God and the restoration of creation.

In the Old Testament, various prophecies and foreshadowings point to a future era of peace and justice under the rule of the Messiah. Prophecies such as those found in Isaiah, Micah, and Zechariah envision a time when nations will live in harmony, swords will be turned into plowshares, and the knowledge of God will cover the earth as the waters cover the sea. These passages depict a renewed creation where righteousness and peace abound, setting the stage for the coming of God's kingdom in its fullness.

In the New Testament, Jesus and the apostles further develop the concept of the kingdom of God, portraying it as both a present reality and a future culmination. Jesus' teachings, particularly in the parables and his proclamation of the kingdom, emphasize its transformative power and its ultimate establishment at the end of the age. The Lord's Prayer, which petitions for God's kingdom to come on earth as it is in heaven, reflects the anticipation of a future consummation of God's reign.

Revelation, the final book of the New Testament, provides a visionary glimpse into the thousand-year reign mentioned in Revelation 20. This passage describes a period in which Satan is bound, and Christ and His saints reign on earth, symbolizing a time of victory and vindication for God's people. The imagery in Revelation underscores the ultimate triumph of righteousness over evil and the fulfillment of God's purposes for creation.

Together, these biblical foundations offer a rich tapestry of prophetic expectation and theological reflection on the Millennium. They lay the groundwork for understanding how the Millennium fits within the broader narrative of God's redemptive plan, culminating in the establishment of His kingdom and the end of sin's dominion over the earth.

Interpretations of the Millennium within Christian theology vary significantly, reflecting diverse perspectives on the timing, nature, and significance of Christ's reign and the fulfillment of God's kingdom.

Premillennialism holds that Christ will return to establish a literal thousand-year reign on earth before the final judgment and the renewal of all creation. Proponents of this view anticipate a future age where Christ rules from Jerusalem, fulfilling Old Testament prophecies and bringing about a period of peace and righteousness. Premillennialism emphasizes a distinct period of tribulation followed by Christ's visible and physical return to initiate His reign.

Postmillennialism presents a more optimistic view of the Millennium, suggesting that the spread of the gospel and Christian principles will gradually transform societies and cultures. This transformation will usher in a golden age of peace and justice, paving the way for Christ's eventual return. Postmillennialists interpret the Millennium symbolically as a period of spiritual triumph and societal improvement before the end times and the final judgment.

Amillennialism, in contrast to both Premillennialism and Postmillennialism, interprets the Millennium symbolically rather than as a literal thousand-year reign. Amillennialists understand the thousand years mentioned in Revelation 20 as a metaphorical period that encompasses the entire church age. According to this view, Christ's reign is spiritual and eternal, not confined to a specific earthly timeframe. Amillennialism emphasizes the ongoing spiritual reign of Christ in the hearts of believers and sees the defeat of Satan and the final judgment as events that coincide with Christ's return.

Moreover, the Seventh-day Adventist interpretation of the Millennium aligns closely with historic Premillennialism, emphasizing Christ's literal return to inaugurate a thousand-year reign of peace and righteousness on earth. Seventh-day Adventists see this period as a time when the saints will reign with Christ, and Satan will be bound, unable to deceive the nations. This interpretation is informed by Adventist teachings on biblical prophecy, emphasizing the Second Coming of Christ as imminent and transformative for the world.

These interpretations reflect the diversity of theological perspectives within Christianity regarding the Millennium and its implications for eschatology. Each view offers distinct insights into the relationship between Christ's kingdom, the church's mission, and the ultimate fulfillment of God's purposes for creation.

The concept of the Millennium has been a subject of theological reflection and debate throughout Christian history, evolving in response to biblical interpretation, cultural contexts, and theological developments.

The historical development of millennial views can be traced back to the early church fathers, who interpreted biblical prophecies about Christ's reign in various ways. Early Christians, influenced by Jewish apocalyptic literature, often expected a literal earthly kingdom ushered in by the Messiah. Over time, different interpretations emerged, including allegorical and spiritual understandings of Christ's kingdom.

Key theological debates and discussions surrounding the Millennium have revolved around its timing, nature, and purpose within God's overall plan of redemption. Early church theologians such as Augustine of Hippo introduced amillennial interpretations, viewing the thousand-year reign in Revelation symbolically rather than literally. This approach shaped much of medieval Christian theology, emphasizing the spiritual nature of Christ's kingdom and downplaying expectations of an earthly reign.

During the Protestant Reformation, millennial views underwent renewed scrutiny and diversity. Reformers such as Martin Luther and John Calvin continued to uphold amillennial perspectives, emphasizing the ongoing spiritual reign of Christ. However, with the rise of premillennialism during the 19th century, influenced by biblical prophecy movements and a focus on literal interpretation of scripture, new debates emerged regarding the sequence of end-time events and the role of Israel in God's eschatological plan.

In modern times, theological discussions on the Millennium have expanded to include diverse perspectives within evangelical, Pentecostal, and Adventist traditions. Premillennialism, postmillennialism, and amillennialism continue to be prominent views, each offering distinct insights into the nature of Christ's kingdom and its implications for the church and society. Contemporary debates often focus on interpreting biblical prophecy, understanding the relationship between the church and the world, and anticipating the ultimate fulfillment of God's kingdom in the new heavens and new earth.

The Millennium remains a pivotal concept in Christian eschatology, providing a framework for understanding God's redemptive purposes, the future of humanity, and the ultimate defeat of sin and evil. Its interpretation continues to inspire theological reflection, spiritual anticipation, and hope for believers awaiting the culmination of God's kingdom.

The Millennium holds profound eschatological significance within Christian theology, symbolizing the ultimate triumph of God's kingdom over sin, evil, and all forms of injustice. As a period of Christ's reign on earth, it represents a time of unprecedented peace, justice, and righteousness—a foretaste of the new heavens and new earth.

Central to the eschatological significance of the Millennium is its role in the culmination of God's redemptive plan. Revelation's portrayal of the thousand-year reign (Revelation 20) depicts a period when Satan is bound and Christ rules with His saints, symbolizing the temporary restraint of evil and the establishment of God's kingdom in its fullness. This period is seen as a decisive phase in the ongoing battle against sin and the restoration of creation to its original harmony and purity.

Christ's return plays a pivotal role in the final defeat of evil during the Millennium. His second coming is anticipated as the moment when He will decisively conquer all opposition, judge the living and the dead, and inaugurate the eternal state of righteousness and peace. The Millennium serves as a transitional period leading to the new heavens and new earth, where God's presence will dwell among His people, and there will be no more death, mourning, or pain (Revelation 21:1-4). Moreover, the heavenly New Jerusalem descends to earth, symbolizing the culmination of the Millennium and the beginning of the new heavens and earth.

Thus, the Millennium represents not only a time of earthly fulfillment of God's promises but also a glimpse into the eternal realities of His kingdom. It underscores the ultimate victory of Christ over sin and evil, offering hope and assurance to believers that God's purposes will be fully realized in His perfect timing. As Christians anticipate the Millennium, they are encouraged to live faithfully, proclaiming the gospel and participating in God's mission to bring about His kingdom on earth as it is in heaven.

The concept of the Millennium carries significant practical implications for how Christians live out their faith and engage with the world around them. These implications extend beyond theoretical understanding to practical applications that shape daily living and mission.

Living with hope and expectation is central to embracing the Millennium's promise of Christ's return and the establishment of God's kingdom in its fullness. Believers are called to maintain a perspective of hopefulness, eagerly anticipating the fulfillment of God's promises while living with a sense of readiness for Christ's imminent return. This hope serves as a source of encouragement and perseverance in times of trial and uncertainty, anchoring believers in the assurance of God's faithfulness.

The Millennium also impacts mission and witness by framing the church's role in advancing God's kingdom on earth. Understanding the Millennium as a period of peace and justice motivates Christians to actively participate in God's mission to reconcile humanity to Himself and restore broken relationships. Believers are called to proclaim the gospel boldly, engage in acts of mercy and justice, and work towards societal transformation that reflects God's kingdom values. The hope of the Millennium inspires a holistic approach to mission that addresses spiritual, social, and cultural dimensions of human need.

Preparation for Christ's return is another practical implication drawn from the concept of the Millennium. Believers are exhorted to live holy and righteous lives, faithfully stewarding the gifts and resources entrusted to them by God. This includes cultivating a vibrant prayer life, nurturing spiritual disciplines, and fostering a community of faith that supports one another in discipleship and growth. The anticipation of Christ's return motivates believers to prioritize eternal values over temporal concerns, living in alignment with God's will and purpose for their lives.

In summary, the Millennium challenges Christians to live with hope and expectation, engage in transformative mission and witness, and diligently prepare for Christ's imminent return. These practical implications encourage a vibrant and purposeful Christian life that reflects God's kingdom values and anticipates the fulfillment of His redemptive plan in the coming age.

Throughout this chapter, we have explored the multifaceted concept of the Millennium and its profound implications within Christian theology and eschatology. From its biblical foundations to diverse theological interpretations, the Millennium signifies a future age of peace, justice, and the ultimate triumph of God's kingdom over sin and evil.

We began by examining the biblical foundations of the Millennium, tracing its roots from Old Testament prophecies to New Testament teachings and Revelation's visionary depiction of Christ's thousand-year reign. These scriptures provide a rich tapestry of hope and anticipation for believers, pointing towards a future where God's sovereignty will be fully realized on earth.

Interpretations of the Millennium—whether premillennial, postmillennial, amillennial, or Seventh-day Adventist—reveal the diversity of perspectives on Christ's reign and the fulfillment of God's promises. Each view contributes unique insights into how Christians understand and anticipate the future manifestation of God's kingdom.

The eschatological significance of the Millennium underscores its pivotal role in the culmination of God's redemptive plan. As a period when Christ will reign visibly and tangibly on earth, the Millennium symbolizes the final defeat of sin and the establishment of eternal peace. This hope encourages believers to live with a sense of expectancy and readiness for Christ's imminent return, steadfast in their faith and commitment to God's kingdom purposes.

In anticipation of the Millennium, believers are encouraged to cultivate lives marked by hope, faithfulness, and diligent preparation. The promise of Christ's return motivates us to live holy and purposeful lives, actively participating in God's mission to bring about His kingdom on earth. As we await the fulfillment of God's promises, we find assurance in the ultimate triumph over sin and evil that Christ's reign will bring—a victory that assures us of our eternal inheritance and the fulfillment of God's perfect plan.

May our hearts be stirred with hope and anticipation as we await the glorious day when Christ will reign supreme, and may we live each day in faithful expectation of His kingdom come and His will be done on earth as it is in heaven.

14. The Renewed Creation

The purpose of this chapter is to delve into the profound and awe-inspiring concept of the New Earth, a renewed creation promised in the Bible. This chapter aims to explore the significance of the New Earth, shedding light on its theological, spiritual, and eschatological dimensions. By examining scriptural references and theological interpretations, we will uncover the promise of a restored world where sin, suffering, and death are no more. The chapter seeks to provide a comprehensive understanding of the New Earth, drawing from biblical texts and Christian thought to illuminate its profound implications for believers.

This chapter will offer an overview of the key concepts related to the New Earth. Central to this exploration is the promise of a new creation as described in the Bible, particularly in the books of Isaiah, Revelation, and other prophetic writings. The New Earth signifies a divine restoration, a return to the original perfection of creation before the fall of humanity. It embodies the fulfillment of God's redemptive plan, where the physical and spiritual realms are harmoniously united under His sovereign reign.

The New Earth holds significant theological and spiritual implications. It represents the culmination of God's promises and the ultimate hope for believers. In this renewed creation, God's presence is intimately experienced, and His glory is fully manifested. The New Earth is depicted as a place of eternal joy, peace, and communion with God, free from the brokenness and pain that characterize our current existence. This chapter will explore the nature of this transformed reality, considering its physical, relational, and spiritual aspects.

Additionally, the chapter will examine the significance of the New Earth in the broader context of Christian eschatology. It serves as the final destination for redeemed humanity, the ultimate fulfillment of God's kingdom. This renewed creation underscores the hope and assurance that believers hold, knowing that their faith in Christ leads to an eternal future in the presence of God. By understanding the New Earth, Christians gain a deeper appreciation of their eschatological hope and the profound implications of God's redemptive work.

In summary, this chapter seeks to provide a thorough exploration of the New Earth, its biblical foundation, theological significance, and eschatological implications. Through this study, readers will gain a deeper understanding of the renewed creation promised by God, offering a vision of hope and restoration that inspires and strengthens their faith.

The New Earth is a concept rooted in Christian eschatology, representing the culmination of God's redemptive plan for creation. It is described as a renewed and perfected world that emerges after the final judgment, where sin, suffering, and death are eradicated, and the presence of God is fully realized. The New Earth is not merely a restoration of the current world but a transformation into a new, glorious state that surpasses human understanding. It signifies the ultimate fulfillment of God's promises to His people, offering a vision of eternal peace, joy, and communion with Him.

The biblical foundation for the New Earth is primarily found in the prophetic and apocalyptic literature of the Bible. In Isaiah 65:17, God declares, "See, I will create new heavens and a new earth. The former things will not be remembered, nor will they come to mind." This prophecy speaks of a divine act of creation that ushers in a new reality, one where the sorrows and pains of the past are forgotten. Similarly, in Revelation 21:1-4, John describes his vision of a new heaven and a new earth, where God dwells among His people, and "He will wipe every tear from their eyes. There will be no more death or mourning or crying or pain, for the old order of things has passed away." These passages provide a glimpse into the nature of the New Earth, emphasizing its transformative and restorative aspects.

Comparing the New Earth with the current earth highlights the profound changes that are to come. The current earth is marked by the consequences of sin, including suffering, environmental degradation, and the inevitability of death. It is a world where humans experience separation from God and one another, leading to various forms of brokenness and discord. The New Earth, in contrast, is depicted as a place where these realities are no longer present. It is a world characterized by the fullness of God's presence, where harmony, peace, and righteousness prevail.

The New Earth also signifies the restoration of the physical creation. In Romans 8:19-21, Paul speaks of creation's eager longing for liberation from its "bondage to decay" and entry into "the freedom and glory of the children of God." This indicates that the renewal of the earth is not just a spiritual or metaphorical event but involves the tangible transformation of the physical world. The New Earth will be a place of beauty and abundance, free from the corruption and decay that afflict the current world.

Moreover, the relational and communal aspects of life on the New Earth will be profoundly different. Relationships will be characterized by perfect love, unity, and fellowship with God and one another. The barriers that divide people in the current world—such as sin, misunderstanding, and conflict—will be removed. In the New Earth, humanity will experience the fullness of community and the joy of living in harmony with God's creation.

In essence, the New Earth represents the ultimate realization of God's redemptive plan, a world where His glory is fully revealed, and His purposes are perfectly fulfilled. It is a vision of hope that contrasts sharply with the present realities of a fallen world, offering believers the assurance of a future where all things are made new. Through this understanding, Christians are encouraged to live with an eternal perspective, anticipating the day when they will dwell in the presence of God on the New Earth.

The restoration of the New Earth is a central theme in Christian eschatology, promising a future where God's original intent for creation is fully realized. This restoration is marked by the renewal and perfection of all things, culminating in a world free from sin, suffering, and death. Understanding the timing of this restoration and the biblical promises and prophecies that underscore it provides believers with a profound sense of hope and anticipation.

The timing of the restoration of the New Earth is intertwined with the events of the end times as described in biblical prophecy. According to Christian eschatological belief, the restoration occurs after the final judgment, which follows the Second Coming of Christ. This sequence of events is laid out in passages such as Revelation 20-21, where the Apostle John describes a vision of the end times. After Satan is defeated and the dead are judged according to their deeds, John sees a new heaven and a new earth, for the first heaven and the first earth have passed away. This indicates that the restoration of the New Earth is a climactic event that follows the resolution of all cosmic and human history.

Biblical promises and prophecies provide a rich tapestry of imagery and assurance regarding the restoration of the New Earth. In the Old Testament, the prophet Isaiah offers a vision of a new creation where the former troubles are forgotten. Isaiah 65:17-25 depicts a world of joy and harmony, where the natural world is at peace, and human life is characterized by longevity and fulfillment. This prophetic vision conveys God's intention to renew and perfect His creation, restoring it to a state of Edenic bliss.

In the New Testament, the promise of the New Earth is reaffirmed through the teachings of Jesus and the writings of the apostles. Jesus speaks of the renewal of all things in Matthew 19:28, indicating that the Kingdom of God involves a comprehensive restoration. The Apostle Peter echoes this in Acts 3:21, referring to a time when God will restore everything as He promised long ago through His holy prophets. These passages emphasize that the restoration of the New Earth is not an isolated event but the fulfillment of a divine promise woven throughout the entire biblical narrative.

The book of Revelation offers the most detailed depiction of the New Earth and its restoration. In Revelation 21-22, John describes a vision of a new heaven and a new earth, where the holy city, the New Jerusalem, comes down from heaven. This city is a symbol of God's presence among His people, radiating His glory and providing a place where there is no more death, mourning, crying, or pain. The imagery of the river of life and the tree of life in Revelation 22:1-2 harks back to the Garden of Eden, signifying a return to the paradise that was lost through sin. This restoration is comprehensive, affecting not only humanity but the entire cosmos, reflecting God's intent to make all things new.

The biblical promises and prophecies about the restoration of the New Earth provide a profound assurance to believers. They highlight God's unwavering commitment to His creation and His plan to bring it to its intended perfection. This hope of restoration encourages Christians to live with an eternal perspective, looking forward to the fulfillment of God's promises and the complete renewal of creation.

In summary, the restoration of the New Earth is a pivotal aspect of Christian eschatology, marking the culmination of God's redemptive plan. The timing of this restoration is associated with the events of the end times, particularly the Second Coming of Christ and the final judgment. The biblical promises and prophecies regarding this restoration offer a rich and detailed vision of a world renewed and perfected, free from the ravages of sin and filled with the presence and glory of God. Through these promises, believers are given a glimpse of the ultimate hope and assurance that awaits them, inspiring faith and anticipation for the new creation.

The characteristics of the New Earth are vividly described in biblical texts and have been the subject of rich theological reflection. These descriptions and reflections provide believers with a profound vision of what the renewed creation will be like, emphasizing its perfection and renewal as key attributes.

Biblical texts offer several detailed descriptions of the New Earth, portraying it as a place of unparalleled beauty, harmony, and divine presence. In Revelation 21-22, the Apostle John's vision includes the New Jerusalem, descending from heaven, adorned like a bride for her husband. This city represents the ultimate dwelling place of God with humanity, where He will wipe every tear from their eyes, and there will be no more death or mourning or crying or pain.

The physical descriptions include streets of pure gold, as transparent as glass, and gates made of single pearls, symbolizing purity and magnificence. The river of the water of life flows from the throne of God and the Lamb, flanked by the tree of life, bearing twelve kinds of fruit and healing the nations. This imagery conveys a sense of abundance, healing, and eternal life.

Isaiah 65:17-25 also provides a rich description of the New Earth, depicting it as a place where people will live in joy and peace. The natural world will be transformed, with the wolf and the lamb feeding together, and the lion eating straw like the ox. This harmonious coexistence of creatures reflects a return to the Edenic state, where creation is free from violence and predation. Human life on the New Earth will be marked by longevity and fulfillment, where people will build houses and dwell in them, plant vineyards and eat their fruit, enjoying the fruits of their labor in a world of justice and prosperity.

Theological reflections on the New Earth emphasize its perfection and renewal. The New Earth is seen as the ultimate realization of God's creative and redemptive purposes, where His glory is fully manifested, and His will is perfectly done. This renewed creation is free from the corruption and decay that characterize the current world, reflecting the transformative power of God's redemption. In this perfected state, the physical, relational, and spiritual aspects of life are restored to their intended harmony.

Perfection on the New Earth is understood not merely as the absence of sin and suffering but as the presence of complete fulfillment and flourishing. Theologians highlight that in the New Earth, humanity will experience the fullness of communion with God, enjoying His presence in a way that is only partially possible in the current world. This communion will be the source of eternal joy, peace, and satisfaction, as believers live in the light of God's glory and love.

Renewal on the New Earth is comprehensive, affecting all dimensions of existence. It involves the restoration of the physical world to a state of beauty and abundance, where creation is liberated from its bondage to decay and brought into the freedom and glory of the children of God, as described in Romans 8:21. This renewal also encompasses the relational aspects of life, where human relationships are characterized by perfect love, unity, and mutual flourishing. The barriers that divide people, such as sin, misunderstanding, and conflict, will be removed, enabling harmonious and fulfilling relationships.

Spiritually, the renewal of the New Earth signifies the culmination of God's redemptive work, where His kingdom is fully realized. Believers will worship and serve God in a creation that is wholly aligned with His purposes, experiencing the fullness of life in His presence. The New Earth represents the final victory of God over sin, death, and evil, a place where His justice, peace, and righteousness prevail eternally.

In summary, the characteristics of the New Earth, as described in biblical texts and theological reflections, highlight its perfection and renewal. This renewed creation is a place of unparalleled beauty, harmony, and divine presence, where God's redemptive purposes are fully realized. The vision of the New Earth offers believers a profound hope and anticipation for the future, inspiring them to live in light of the ultimate fulfillment of God's promises.

The concept of the New Earth is deeply rooted in the narrative of the problem of sin and the fall, as well as God's plan for redemption and restoration. Understanding these foundational reasons helps illuminate why the New Earth is necessary and how it fits into the broader scope of God's redemptive purposes.

The problem of sin and the fall is the starting point for understanding the need for a New Earth. According to the biblical account, sin entered the world through the disobedience of Adam and Eve in the Garden of Eden, as described in Genesis 3.

This act of rebellion against God's command resulted in a fundamental fracture in the relationship between God and humanity, as well as a curse upon the entire creation. Sin brought about spiritual death, alienation from God, and a pervasive corruption that affected every aspect of life. The consequences of the fall are seen in the pain, suffering, and decay that characterize the current world. The creation, which was initially declared "very good" by God, became subject to futility and groaning under the weight of sin, as depicted in Romans 8:20-22.

In response to the problem of sin and the fall, God's plan for redemption and restoration unfolds throughout the biblical narrative. From the moment of humanity's disobedience, God initiated a plan to redeem and restore His creation. This plan is seen in His covenant with Abraham, the giving of the Law to Moses, the messages of the prophets, and ultimately, the coming of Jesus Christ. Central to God's redemptive plan is the life, death, and resurrection of Jesus, who came to reconcile humanity to God and to undo the effects of sin. Through His sacrificial death on the cross, Jesus bore the penalty for sin and opened the way for humanity to be restored to a right relationship with God.

The redemption achieved through Christ is not limited to individuals but extends to the entire creation. The New Testament repeatedly affirms that God's plan encompasses the renewal of all things. In Ephesians 1:10, Paul speaks of God's purpose to bring unity to all things in heaven and on earth under Christ. This cosmic scope of redemption points to the ultimate goal of God's plan: the restoration of creation to its original perfection. The New Earth, therefore, is the culmination of this redemptive plan, where the effects of sin are fully reversed, and creation is restored to its intended state.

God's plan for the New Earth is also a demonstration of His faithfulness to His promises. Throughout the Bible, God promises to make all things new, to wipe away every tear, and to establish a kingdom of peace, justice, and righteousness. These promises find their ultimate fulfillment in the New Earth, where God's presence is fully manifested, and His purposes are perfectly realized. The New Earth is a place where God dwells with His people, where there is no more death, mourning, crying, or pain, as described in Revelation 21:3-4. It is a world where the harmony of Eden is restored, and the glory of God is fully revealed.

The New Earth also reflects the depth of God's love and grace. Despite humanity's rebellion and the widespread effects of sin, God's desire to restore and renew His creation underscores His unwavering commitment to His creation. The New Earth is a testament to God's transformative power, capable of bringing life out of death, beauty out of brokenness, and joy out of sorrow. It is a vision of hope that assures believers that no matter how marred the current world may be by sin, God's redemptive purposes will ultimately prevail.

In essence, the reasons for the New Earth are deeply intertwined with the problem of sin and the fall, and God's comprehensive plan for redemption and restoration. The New Earth addresses the consequences of sin, fulfills God's redemptive promises, and showcases His love and grace. It represents the ultimate hope for believers, affirming that God's purposes for His creation will be realized in a renewed and perfected world where His presence and glory are fully manifested.

The eschatological perspectives on the New Earth involve understanding its relationship with the Millennium and the end of sin, as well as its connection to biblical prophecy. These aspects are crucial for a comprehensive view of the New Earth within the broader framework of Christian eschatology, offering insights into how the final stages of God's redemptive plan unfold.

The relationship between the New Earth and the Millennium is a significant aspect of eschatological thought. The Millennium, described in Revelation 20, is a period of a thousand years during which Christ reigns on earth with His saints. This era is characterized by peace, justice, and the binding of Satan, who is temporarily restrained from deceiving the nations.

Various interpretations exist regarding the nature and timing of the Millennium. Premillennialism views the Millennium as a future literal reign of Christ on earth before the final judgment, whereas postmillennialism and amillennialism interpret the Millennium symbolically, as either a golden age brought about by the church's influence or a present spiritual reign of Christ.

In premillennial thought, the New Earth follows the Millennium and the final defeat of Satan. After the thousand-year reign, Satan is released for a short time, leading to a final rebellion, which is swiftly crushed. This event is followed by the final judgment, where the dead are judged according to their deeds. Revelation 20:11-15 describes this judgment scene, culminating in the destruction of death and Hades in the lake of fire. With the eradication of all evil, the stage is set for the creation of the New Earth, where God's people will dwell eternally in His presence.

The end of sin is a crucial element in understanding the New Earth. The eradication of sin and its consequences is a central theme in the eschatological vision. In Revelation 21:4, it is proclaimed that in the New Earth, there will be no more death, mourning, crying, or pain, for the old order of things has passed away. This signifies the complete and final end of sin and its effects. The New Earth is depicted as a place of perfect holiness and righteousness, where nothing impure will ever enter, and only those whose names are written in the Lamb's book of life will dwell there (Revelation 21:27).

The connection to biblical prophecy is essential for understanding the New Earth. Prophetic literature in both the Old and New Testaments points toward a future renewal of creation. In Isaiah 65:17-25, the prophet envisions a new heaven and a new earth, where former things are not remembered, and joy and peace prevail. This prophecy highlights a restored creation where harmony is restored among all living beings, reflecting a return to the peace of Eden.

In the New Testament, Jesus speaks of the renewal of all things in Matthew 19:28, indicating a comprehensive restoration associated with His second coming. The Apostle Paul also addresses this theme in Romans 8:19-21, describing creation's eager expectation for the children of God to be revealed and liberated from its bondage to decay. These passages underscore the hope of a future transformation that encompasses all creation.

The book of Revelation provides the most detailed prophetic vision of the New Earth. John's apocalyptic vision reveals the final victory of God over evil and the establishment of a new, eternal order. Revelation 21-22 describes the New Jerusalem, the holy city, coming down from heaven, symbolizing the ultimate fulfillment of God's redemptive plan. This vision includes vivid imagery of a renewed creation, with the river of the water of life, the tree of life, and the throne of God and the Lamb. It portrays a world where God dwells with His people, illuminating the connection between the New Earth and the fulfillment of biblical prophecy.

In summary, eschatological perspectives on the New Earth involve its relationship with the Millennium and the end of sin, as well as its connection to biblical prophecy. The Millennium represents a pivotal phase in the unfolding of God's redemptive plan, leading to the final defeat of evil and the creation of the New Earth. The New Earth signifies the ultimate eradication of sin and the fulfillment of prophetic visions of a restored and perfected creation. These perspectives provide believers with a comprehensive understanding of the New Earth within the broader context of Christian eschatology, offering a profound hope for the future.

The promise of the New Earth has profound practical implications for Christian living, shaping how believers understand their present responsibilities and future hope. Living in anticipation of the New Earth and embracing stewardship of creation and environmental ethics are key aspects of this transformative vision.

Living in anticipation of the New Earth calls Christians to adopt an eternal perspective that influences their daily lives. The certainty of a renewed creation where God's justice, peace, and righteousness reign encourages believers to live in a manner consistent with the values of God's kingdom. This anticipation fosters a sense of hope and perseverance, motivating Christians to endure present hardships with the assurance of future glory. The Apostle Paul captures this sentiment in Romans 8:18, stating that the sufferings of this present time are not worth comparing with the glory that is to be revealed. This hope not only provides comfort but also inspires a commitment to holiness, love, and service, reflecting the character of Christ and the reality of the coming kingdom.

Furthermore, living in anticipation of the New Earth involves a proactive engagement with the world. Christians are called to be agents of God's redemption, working toward justice, reconciliation, and peace in their communities. This active participation in God's redemptive work mirrors the ultimate restoration that the New Earth represents. Believers are encouraged to live out the values of the coming kingdom, promoting righteousness, compassion, and integrity in their personal and social lives. By doing so, they provide a foretaste of the New Earth, embodying the transformative power of God's kingdom in the present.

The stewardship of creation is another vital implication of the promise of the New Earth. The biblical mandate for humanity to care for the earth, as articulated in Genesis 1:28, underscores the responsibility to steward God's creation wisely and lovingly. This stewardship is grounded in the recognition that the earth is the Lord's, and humans are entrusted with its care. The hope of a renewed creation amplifies this responsibility, calling Christians to protect and preserve the environment as an act of worship and obedience to God.

Environmental ethics, informed by the vision of the New Earth, emphasize the interconnectedness of all creation and the importance of sustainable living. Christians are called to adopt practices that promote the health and flourishing of the natural world, recognizing that their actions have a direct impact on the environment. This involves reducing waste, conserving resources, and advocating for policies that protect the ecosystem. By doing so, believers honor God's creation and align themselves with His redemptive purposes.

The hope of the New Earth also challenges Christians to confront environmental injustice, advocating for the well-being of marginalized communities disproportionately affected by environmental degradation. This commitment to justice reflects the biblical call to love one's neighbor and to seek the common good. Environmental stewardship thus becomes a tangible expression of faith, demonstrating love for God, care for creation, and compassion for humanity.

In summary, the practical implications of the promise of the New Earth for Christian living are multifaceted and transformative. Living in anticipation of the New Earth involves adopting an eternal perspective that shapes daily life, fostering hope, perseverance, and active engagement in God's redemptive work. The stewardship of creation and environmental ethics, grounded in the biblical mandate and the vision of a renewed creation, call Christians to care for the earth responsibly and to promote justice and sustainability. By embracing these practical implications, believers participate in God's redemptive purposes, embodying the hope and values of the coming kingdom in their present lives.

The concept of the New Earth in Christian theology can be enriched by examining it alongside other eschatological views from different religious traditions. This comparative approach highlights both similarities and differences, offering a broader understanding of how diverse faiths envision the ultimate destiny of the world and humanity.

In Christianity, the New Earth represents the culmination of God's redemptive plan, characterized by the renewal of creation and the establishment of a perfect, eternal dwelling place for God's people. This eschatological vision includes the complete eradication of sin, suffering, and death, and the presence of God dwelling with humanity in a restored creation. The Christian hope for the New Earth is deeply rooted in biblical prophecies and the teachings of Jesus and the apostles, particularly as seen in the book of Revelation.

In contrast, Islamic eschatology, while sharing some common elements with Christianity, offers a different perspective on the end times and the afterlife. In Islam, the Day of Judgment (Yawm al-Qiyamah) is a central concept, where all individuals are resurrected and judged by Allah based on their deeds. The righteous are rewarded with eternal life in Jannah (Paradise), a place of unimaginable beauty and pleasure, while the wicked face eternal punishment in Jahannam (Hell). Islamic eschatology emphasizes moral accountability and the ultimate justice of Allah, but it does not specifically describe a renewed earth akin to the Christian New Earth. Instead, the focus is on the eternal abode of the faithful in a paradisiacal state.

Judaism also offers a rich eschatological tradition, though its views on the afterlife and the end times vary among different sects and historical periods. Traditional Jewish eschatology anticipates the coming of the Messiah (Mashiach), who will usher in an era of peace, justice, and divine presence. This Messianic Age includes the ingathering of the exiles, the rebuilding of the Temple in Jerusalem, and the establishment of God's kingdom on earth. While there is a strong emphasis on the renewal of the world and the restoration of Israel, Jewish eschatology tends to focus more on the present world and the collective destiny of the Jewish people rather than a completely new creation.

Hindu eschatology presents a cyclical view of time, characterized by endless cycles of creation, preservation, and destruction (samsara). Each cycle, or yuga, eventually leads to the dissolution of the world and its subsequent rebirth. The ultimate goal in Hinduism is moksha, the liberation from the cycle of rebirth and union with the divine. While Hindu eschatology involves a transformation of the soul and its reunion with the divine essence, it differs significantly from the linear, restorative vision of a New Earth found in Christianity.

Buddhist eschatology also differs markedly from the Christian concept of the New Earth. Buddhism teaches the impermanence of all things and the cyclical nature of existence. The ultimate goal is Nirvana, the cessation of suffering and liberation from the cycle of rebirth. While there are various cosmological beliefs about different realms of existence, the focus is on attaining enlightenment and escaping the cycle of samsara rather than on the renewal of the physical world.

Despite these differences, there are noteworthy similarities across these religious perspectives. Most eschatological views emphasize a future transformation, whether it is the renewal of creation, the attainment of paradise, or liberation from the cycle of rebirth. They also share a common concern with justice, moral accountability, and the ultimate triumph of good over evil.

The differences, however, are significant and reflect the unique theological frameworks and worldviews of each tradition. Christianity's linear narrative of creation, fall, redemption, and restoration contrasts with the cyclical patterns found in Hinduism and Buddhism. The personal, relational nature of the Christian God, who dwells with His people in the New Earth, differs from the more impersonal ultimate realities in some Eastern traditions.

In summary, comparing the Christian vision of the New Earth with other eschatological views reveals both shared themes and distinctive differences. While various religious traditions envision a future transformation and emphasize justice and moral accountability, their specific eschatological expectations and understandings of ultimate reality reflect their unique theological and philosophical foundations. This comparative perspective enriches our understanding of the diverse ways in which humanity seeks to comprehend and anticipate the end of the world and the fulfillment of ultimate hope.

The concept of the New Earth encapsulates the culmination of God's redemptive plan, promising a future where creation is restored to its intended perfection and harmony. Throughout this chapter, we have explored various dimensions of this profound eschatological hope, delving into its biblical foundations, theological implications, and practical significance for Christian living.

We began by defining the New Earth and contrasting it with the current world marred by sin and decay. This comparison highlighted the transformative nature of God's promise, envisioning a world free from suffering, pain, and death, where God's presence is fully realized. The restoration of the New Earth, grounded in biblical promises and prophecies, underscores the timing and certainty of this ultimate renewal. Theological reflections on the characteristics of the New Earth revealed a creation marked by unparalleled beauty, peace, and the fullness of life in God's presence.

We also considered the reasons for the New Earth, rooted in the problem of sin and the fall, and God's comprehensive plan for redemption and restoration. The eradication of sin and the fulfillment of God's redemptive promises affirm His unwavering commitment to His creation. Eschatological perspectives further illuminated the relationship between the New Earth, the Millennium, and biblical prophecy, offering a broader understanding of how these final stages unfold.

Practical implications for Christian living were examined, emphasizing the importance of living in anticipation of the New Earth and embracing stewardship of creation. Believers are called to embody the values of God's kingdom, promoting justice, righteousness, and sustainability in their daily lives. Comparative theology provided a broader context, highlighting similarities and differences with other religious eschatological views, enriching our understanding of the diverse ways humanity envisions the ultimate destiny of the world.

In reflecting on these key points, believers are encouraged to hold fast to the hope of the New Earth, allowing this vision to inspire and guide their lives. This anticipation provides a profound sense of purpose, motivating Christians to live in alignment with God's redemptive purposes and to actively participate in His work of restoration. The promise of the New Earth assures believers that their present struggles and efforts are not in vain but are part of a larger divine narrative that culminates in ultimate fulfillment.

Final reflections on the New Earth remind us of the depth of God's love and grace, capable of transforming a broken world into a place of perfect peace and joy. This ultimate restoration reflects God's faithfulness to His promises and His desire for a harmonious relationship with His creation. The vision of the New Earth serves as a beacon of hope, calling believers to live with an eternal perspective and to trust in the certainty of God's redemptive plan.

As we conclude this exploration of the New Earth, let us hold firmly to this hope, allowing it to shape our lives and actions. In anticipation of the New Earth, we are called to live as faithful stewards of creation, embodying the values of God's kingdom and working towards the renewal of all things. This eschatological hope offers a profound source of encouragement and inspiration, assuring us of the ultimate restoration and fulfillment that awaits in the presence of our loving and sovereign God.

TRUE PRINCIPLES OF CHRISTIANITY BOOK TWO

REQUEST FREE BIBLE STUDY GUIDES AT:
Call: 1-888-456-7933
Request Free Bible Guides at:
www.BibleSchools.com
Study online at:
www.BibleSchools.com
Discover
P.O. Box 999
Loveland, CO 80539-0999
IT IS WRITTEN
Call: 1-844-WRITTEN
1-844- 974-8836
Write:
PO Box 6
Chattanooga, TN 37401-0006
For Online Interactive Bible Studies:
www.itiswritten.study